CREATIVE PASTORAL CARE AND COUNSELING

WOMAN-BATTERING

Carol J. Adams

FORTRESS PRESS   MINNEAPOLIS

for Bruce, my care provider

WOMAN-BATTERING

Copyright ©1994 Augsburg Fortress. All rights reserved. Except for brief quotations in critical articles or reviews, no part of this book may be reproduced in any manner without prior written permission from the publisher. Write to: Permissions, Augsburg Fortress, 426 S. Fifth St., Box 1209, Minneapolis, MN 55440.

Scripture quotations unless otherwise noted are from the New Revised Standard Version Bible, copyright ©1989 by the Division of Christian Education of the National Council of the Churches of Christ in the United States of America.

This publication is designed to provide accurate and authoritative information in regard to the subject matter covered. It is sold with the understanding that the publisher is not engaged in rendering legal, accounting, or other professional services. If legal advice or other expert assistance is required, the services of a competent professional person should be sought. *From a Declaration of Principles jointly adopted by the Committee of the American Bar Association and a Committee of Publishers.*

Excerpts and "Signs of Abuse" data from *When Love Goes Wrong*, copyright © 1992 Ann Jones and Susan Schechter. Reprinted by permission of HarperCollins Publishers, Inc.

Table "Assessing Whether Batterers Will Kill" is from *Seeking Justice: Legal Advocacy Principles and Practice*, copyright © Barbara Hart and Jan Steuhling. Reprinted by permission.

"Power and Control Wheel" and "Equality Wheel" are reprinted by permission of Domestic Abuse Intervention Project, Duluth, MN.

Credits continued on p. 10

Cover design: Spangler Design Team
Cover art: "Sisters" by Barbara Harman. Used by permission of the artist.

Library of Congress Cataloging-in-Publication Data

Adams, Carol J.
    Woman-battering / Carol J. Adams
       p. cm. — (Creative pastoral care and counseling series)
    Includes bibliographical references.
    ISBN 0-8006-2785-7 (alk. paper)
    1. Abused women—Pastoral counseling of. 2. Church work with abused women. 3. Abusive men—Pastoral counseling of. 4. Church work with abusive men. I. Title. II. Series.
    BV4445.5.A32 1994
    259'.1—dc20   94-9988
                                                   CIP

The paper used in this publication meets the minimum requirements of American National Standard for Information Sciences—Permanence of Paper for Printed Library Materials, ANSI Z329.48-1984. ∞™

Manufactured in U.S.A.   AF 1–2785

98   97   96   95   94   1   2   3   4   5   6   7   8   9   10

CONTENTS

Preface   5

Introduction: Woman-Battering in Christian Congregations?   11

1. Naming   28

2. Being Prepared   46

3. Making Referrals   56

4. Safety   69

5. Accountability   87

6. Suffering and Theology   103

Conclusion: Creating a Responsive Church Community   115

Appendix: Handling an Emergency Call   119

Bibliography   122

Local Resources   127

90462

TABLES

Table 1: Signs of Abuse   40

Table 2: Signs of an Abuser   42

Table 3: Proactive Pastoral Care   67

Table 4: Assessing Whether Batterers Will Kill   76

Table 5: Distinguishing Forgiveness   82

Table 6: Distinguishing Repentance   94

ILLUSTRATIONS

Figure 1: Power and Control Wheel   18

Figure 2: Community Accountability Wheel   61

Figure 3: Equality Wheel   101

Figure 4: Flow Chart for Crisis Calls   121

PREFACE

Ministers—clergy, chaplains, pastoral counselors, deacons—seek to be available to help others, and often they are helpful. Yet, battered women who escape their abusers ranked the helpfulness of the assistance they received from clergy at the bottom (Bowker 1983). Women who turned to their clergy for marital guidance stayed longer with their abusers, and the abuse did not subside (Pagelow 1981, 126).

Picture these not-so-uncommon scenes: A pastor is approached by a woman whose marriage ceremony he performed, and she reports that last night her husband—a respected community figure and church leader—pushed her down the stairs. Or, while making rounds, a hospital chaplain stops in the emergency room to see a pregnant woman, who discloses that her husband kicked her in the groin. Or, a young couple preparing for marriage is referred to a pastoral counselor; in a private session, the woman cautiously shares that her boyfriend slaps her around, but that things will get better when they are married. Or a youth pastor talks with a frightened thirteen year old who sobs that her seventeen-year-old boyfriend choked her and told her that if he could not have her, no one could.

In each scene, the caregiver's actions will have serious consequences for the woman, the man who batters, and the minister. She may be encouraged to consider the relationship rather than her safety, and thus stay with the abuser longer. Without notice that what the assaultive man is doing is wrong, he will continue his behavior. More than a few ministers feel a crisis of inadequacy in the face of such disclosures and with good reason: They have not been prepared for this.

A PRACTICAL RESPONSE

This book was written as a practical response to many ministers who approached me after they did not know what to say to a woman suffering violence from her abusive husband. My focus and audience is the Christian community, and the particular issues that are raised in a Christian context. Although a pastor in a congregational setting is used in most examples, the recommendations can be helpful to hospital and college chaplains, deacons, and youth chaplains as well as pastoral counselors.

5

The focus is on how to respond when men who batter or their victims seek help. Information is provided so that abusers and their victims can be identified and appropriate responses offered. NOTE: Making a referral to a specialized service for victims of battering is essential.

The basic problem is that many ministers feel confident in assisting congregational members to work out basic human relations, even when violence has been introduced. Three questions can determine whether such confidence is well founded:

- Do I understand the life-threatening nature of battering and the control over another that battering establishes?
- Do I understand the importance of ensuring complete confidentiality to a woman so that unless she permits this, her husband not be told that she has talked with me?
- Do I understand that the abuser's version of what happened might be radically different from the victim's version? Am I prepared to challenge his interpretation if counseling with him is an appropriate aspect of my response to her needs?

Answering no to any of these questions indicates that a minister is not ready to assist a battered woman. Errors in counseling would, in a sense, be those of omission, stemming from incomplete knowledge. Reading this book and consulting its bibliography should assist in preparing to help.

Three additional questions can discern whether such confidence is misguided:

- Do I have any beliefs about a woman's role in a marriage that might reinforce the man who batters? For example, do I hold notions that a wife should be obedient to her husband? that he has the final authority?
- Do I believe that a family should be kept together at all costs, even the woman's safety?
- Do I believe that women are there to meet any of my emotional, professional, or sexual needs? For example, do I feel more important when assisting families or when a woman is dependent on me because she places all her trust in me?

Answering yes to any of these questions indicates that a minister is not able to assist a battered woman. Errors in counseling would, in a sense, be those of commission stemming from unhelpful beliefs. Challenging a woman's decision to leave a marriage (either temporarily or permanently) places her back in danger and encourages her abuser who experiences no negative consequences for his criminal behavior. Hold-ing rigid views about women's duty or her place or divorce or the husband's authority—or deriving satisfaction from her lack of confidence—means that the needed resources will be kept from her. Without linkage to these resources, she may be severely injured or murdered. This book cautions against and even counters such views, and it identifies precisely how theological advice is substituted for practical, caring advice.

For many years now, I have consulted with clergy and other pastoral care providers working with abusive men and their partners. I have experienced clergypeople's sincere commitment to be the allies that battered women and their advocates need them to be. Together, ministers and I have strategized issues involving premarital counseling, danger to a child, alcohol abuse and battering. In all these conversations, I have noticed an earnest concern to do the correct thing, to provide adequate guidance over unmapped territory. This earnestness represents the best instincts of ministers, who sincerely wish to help and not be the cause of more harm. This book seeks to build on this desire.

FOCUSING ON WOMEN

I will be discussing victims of battering as women because based on FBI statistics, 95 percent of victims of battering are women. My own experience confirms these findings. In 1978, my minister spouse and I started a hotline for battered women in rural upstate New York: The overwhelming number of calls were from women. Not only are women disproportionately the victims of battering but also the way society responds to women versus men who are victims of battering requires keeping the focus on women.

The cultural context in which ministry occurs in the United States is one in which woman-battering is normative and has not been seen as deviant behavior. In contrast, violence against men in intimate relationships is deviant and society responds to it as such. This is why women are so harshly punished for using violence in self-defense. ("The average sentence for a woman who kills her spouse or companion is fifteen to twenty years, compared to an average sentence of two to six years for a man" ["Developments" 1993, 1575 n. 3].) The reaction to the movie *Thelma and Louise,* and more recently, to the actions of Lorena Bobbitt, demonstrate the furor that greets women who respond with violence. Some men are victims of violence in a relationship. This should be addressed as an individual problem. A man may be injured when a woman strikes back or acts in self-defense. This is not the same as what women experience and should not be confused with woman-battering.

This book's main focus is on victims rather than abusers for three reasons. First, justice means, if nothing else, focusing attention on the needs of victims. Second, victims of woman-battering are more likely to seek out a minister's help than are the abusers. Third, in the face of violence, ensuring safety must be the first goal. Any one attack can be fatal.

Battering is not solely a crisis, it is a chronic situation marked by crisis events. Yet ministers are more prone to focus either on the nature of the crisis and assume that it has passed, or on the nature of the intimate relationship between the abuser and the battered woman and assume that it should continue. What needs attention is the battering behavior.

Inappropriate responses are inappropriate because they endanger victims. In identifying appropriate responses, I have listened to the voices of ministers who have told me with regret of the mistakes they made, the voices of women who escaped an abuser's violence, and the voices of other professionals who work in the field of woman-battering.

Individual pastoral care is not the solution to ending battering behavior. A coordinated community response is. Consistently applied community sanctions for the men who choose violence is absolutely essential. The survivors need a community that offers safety and an opportunity to reflect in safety on the traumatic experiences of being victimized by battering. In holding the abuser accountable, society begins the work of ensuring justice for the victim and offers the possibility of repentance and healing for the abuser.

Some of the material presented here is emotionally distressing, unsettling. Reading about abusive behavior may be discomforting. Learning about physical and psychological harm is difficult. Some people experience headaches, physical exhaustion, and racing pulses when they read of rape, sexual abuse, and battering. Survivors of abuse may experience painful memories of their own abuse.

The alternative to the painful process of becoming educated and prepared is silence. Silence over the years has only meant that the suffering has continued. Silence inevitably sides with the perpetrator and injustice over against the victim and justice. Change is possible, but only when the need for change is named and action undertaken. We must know the facts if we are to help. I have always found it better to learn of intentional harm and cruelty so that I can do something about the abuse, rather than to protect a false naïveté that cannot see and thus does not act.

Many friends, survivors, and ministers provided immense help to me and I wish to express thanks to them for their steadfastness: To my partner Bruce Buchanan who has been invaluable in shaping the pastoral responses developed in this book; to Marie Fortune, who has been a pioneer in this field, a thoughtful friend, and helpful critic of my work; and my editor Timothy Staveteig, who was the midwife for this book. Thanks also to Marjorie Procter-Smith, Pat Davis, Nancy Bickers, Pam Willhoite, and Sarah Bentley who have shared generously their expertise and their attentiveness to this project, including thoughtful readings of earlier versions of this book. Thanks to Jennifer Manlowe, David Switzer, Leigh Nachman Hofheimer, Mary E. Hunt, and Kathleen Carlin for reading the manuscript and providing sensitive criticisms. Dick Bathrick of Men Stopping Violence provided helpful insights into men's helpseeking. I am also greatly indebted to the work of Anne Ganley, Ann Jones, and Susan Schecter. Students in my classes on sexual and domestic violence at Perkins School of Theology have helped me to refine and improve my approach. Special thanks to Marsha Engle-Rowbottom, Marlena Cardenas-Griffin, Barbara Harmon Hill, and Stephen Smith. Tables 5, Distinguishing Forgiveness, and 6, Distinguishing Repentance, were devised by my students Elaine Robinson and Randy Pratt, and are used with their permission. Gene Mason again rescued me from computer difficulties, and the staff of the Richardson Public Library have been unstinting in their assistance.

Conversations with shelter workers over the years have helped me identify recurring theological concerns of battered women. I thank especially Karen Brown, Christiane Dutton, and Susan Kelley. Kathleen Carlin of Men Stopping Violence offered a prophetic stance at a pivotal time; the book is stronger as a result. Jennifer Robertson of AWAKE, David Garvin and Mike Jackson of the Domestic Violence Institute of Michigan, and Chaplain Nancy Allison provided last-minute assistance, which I greatly appreciate.

My parents, Lee Towne and Muriel Adams, have provided personal support over the many years that I have worked on this subject, offering their specialized skills in the law and advocacy. I thank them for sheltering a battered woman when I was growing up, thus teaching me the importance of safety. Virginia and Arthur Buchanan provided yeoman's labor in our home as I struggled to meet deadlines. My thanks to them for creating the time and space for me to work on this book.

INTRODUCTION: WOMAN-BATTERING IN CHRISTIAN CONGREGATIONS?

In many Christian families, the husband abuses his wife. Ministers may have performed the funeral service for a congregational member killed by her husband or for an abusive husband killed by his wife or child. Hospital chaplains are learning that many of the injured women they see sustained these injuries from their husbands. College chaplains and youth ministers meet many young women at risk of being victimized by dating violence.

In the pews of every church every Sunday sit both perpetrators and their victims. They come from all racial and ethnic groups, can be wealthy, middle class, or poor, lawyers or teachers, businesspeople or construction workers. They are Presbyterian, Catholic, Lutheran, Baptist, Church of God in Christ, Unitarian, AME Methodist—in every denomination in the United States.

When a man hits a woman, he has not lost control; he achieves and maintains control. When a woman is hit by her partner, she begins a search not only to achieve safety in the face of violence but also meaning in the face of trauma. Often the result is that she reorganizes her life, attempting appeasement. As the battering continues or escalates despite appeasement, the search for meaning is impaled upon meaninglessness. Thus, she must reorient her theology—a loving God who protects innocent people is often dethroned by a punitive God who requires suffering. This God at least conforms to the victim's experience, dangerously confirming this experience as acceptable.

One shelter worker described a battered woman who told her that her church was her family. Her husband and abuser was a church leader. Her appeals for help from her church family and the pastor received little substantive response. They did not support her need for safety. To them, the sanctity of the marriage was more important than her safety. When her husband went for pastoral help to end his abuse, the church told her that he was working on it. However, she continued to be brutally assaulted by him. She later divorced him—losing all sense of family because the church rebuffed her. After a time, he assured her that he had gotten help, and she returned to him. The day after she returned, he beat her. In the wake of the beating, she committed suicide. What this woman needed is what every battered woman needs: a community to hold her abuser accountable because she could not and spiritual support from her pastor and church. She needed not to have to choose between safety and the support of the church.

11

WHAT IS WOMAN-BATTERING?

Battering is the use of violence or the threat of violence as a means to control another person. Two key aspects of violence are threat and control. That is, the effects of battering are seen not only in the actual physical assaults but also in how fear of being hurt is used to manipulate and control a woman through threats (Carlin, 1).

Battering is both "assaultive behavior occurring in an intimate, sexual, theoretically peer, usually cohabitating relationship," and "a *pattern* of behavior, not isolated individual events. One form of battering builds on another and sets the stage for the next battering episode" (Ganley 1989, 202). Battering is entrenched behavior that establishes domination or control in a relationship.

Battering may be done intentionally to inflict suffering. For example, the man may physically punish a victim for thinking or behaving in a way that is contrary to the perpetrator's views. Or battering may be done simply to establish control in a conversation without intending harm. Regardless of the intent, the violence has the same impact on the victim and on the relationship. It establishes a system of coercive control (203).

Is Battering Really Much of a Problem?

Abusive men are the major source of injury to adult women in the United States. According to U.S. Department of Justice's Bureau of Justice Statistics, "women are six times more likely than men to be the victim of a violent crime committed by an intimate" (Harlow 1991, 1). According to the U.S. Bureau of Justice National Crime Survey, in the United States a woman is beaten in her home every fifteen seconds (1). Testimony before the Senate Judiciary Committee indicates that as many as four million women are affected each year by woman-battering (U.S. Congress, Senate 1990). In the United States, a woman is more likely to be assaulted, injured, raped, or killed by her male partner than by any other assailant. Forty percent of all homeless women and children in this country are fleeing domestic violence (Zorza 1991, 421).

Women physically abused by their husbands are at high risk of sexual assault. Anywhere from one-third to one-half of battered women are victims of marital sexual assault (Finkelhor and Yllo 1985, 22). Although the face and breasts are common sites of assault, during pregnancy, the abdomen is frequently a target for abuse (Hilberman 1980, 1340). Women abused by their male partners are twice as likely to miscarry than women who are not abused. The March of Dimes has concluded that battering of women during pregnancy is the number one cause of birth defects.

In What Ways Are Women Battered?

The behavior of men who hurt women includes threats, reckless driving, throwing and damaging possessions, the injuring or killing of pets, burning, punching, kicking, barring her exit, keeping a woman awake against her will, throwing a woman down the stairs, sexual humiliation, rape.

Men who batter choke their partners, hit them, shove and push them, throw things at them, beat their heads against a wall or the floor, pull out their hair, refuse to allow them to get medical care, threaten them with weapons, push them out of moving cars, kidnap them. They wipe up milk they spilled on the floor with their wives' hair, they force their wives to lick the floor, to eat from a pet's dish, to have sex with the family dog. Men stab, cut, shoot, and pistol-whip their wives or female partners. As one woman said "anything handy" becomes an abuser's weapon. (For a list of objects, see Stacey and Shupe 1983, 58–59.)

Women are often raped as a continuation of the beating, threatened with more violence if they fail to comply with their husband's sexual requests, or forced to have sex to oblige the abuser's need to make up after a beating. Batterers who also rape their wives committed some of the most brutal and violent assaults. Women who survived battering rapes often felt that it was the sexual abuse that was the most devastating.

In What Ways Is Battering Dangerous and Abusive?

To determine whether particular acts of battering are dangerous, the attempt is made to place them on some sort of severity continuum. This, however, is not helpful. "The reality is that shoving can be as or more dangerous than punching when evaluated by the injury to the victim. A person who is shoved may be paralyzed or killed, while a person who is punched may receive a broken nose" (Ganley 1981, 9–10). Bonnie Burstow points out that

> the assumption is that the greater the physical damage, the worse the abuse. This popular image leaves out as much as it shows, and the assumption itself is naive. On the purely physical side, some subtler acts deeply harm because of their psychological impact. These include:
> • Subtle disfigurement of any part of the body that the woman takes special pride in or identifies with.
> • Subtle disfigurement to any part of the body that the woman is already ashamed of.
> • Being held firmly by some part of the body. (1992, 150)

Battering is life-threatening behavior; a single attack can leave the victim dead or seriously injured. Women abused by their male partners must be ever vigilant against future violence. One study of women housed in battered women's shelters in Texas found that 67 percent of the batterers had threatened to kill their victims and 41 percent of the victims had been abused with weapons or objects (Gondolf and Fisher 1988, 6). Most women on trial for homicide had been battered by the men they killed. Every six hours—four times a day—a woman is killed by her male partner. Almost daily, a man kills a woman who has left him because of his physical abuse of her. Of all women killed in the United States, 30 percent were murdered by their current or former male partners ("Developments" 1993). An estimated 25 to 35 percent of all visits by women to emergency rooms are for injuries suffered at the hands of their male partners or ex-partners. In short—as many professionals who work with men who batter emphasize—"any man who batters must be considered dangerous" (Stordeur and Stille 1989, 108).

Why Do Men Batter?

Generally speaking, battering is not a character defect or a sign of mental illness. Nor is it a universal practice in intimate relationships. But as a behavior that establishes the perpetrator's control and dominance, nothing functions as effectively as battering.

Professionals who work with men who batter have observed that assaultive men believe stereotypes about male-female roles and overidentify with the stereotypic male role. Because of this overidentification they feel the right to control anyone with less power or status (women and children). As a result, "husband-dominance is also a predictor of child abuse" (Bowker et al. 1988, 165). Husbands think that authority is their privilege, and may expect male clergy and counselors to affirm this in terms of their traditional ideas about sex roles. The inflexible adherence to traditional expectations for men in relation to women is one of the forces that makes wives "appropriate victims" (see Dobash and Dobash 1979, 31–47).

Does stress cause battering? Stress does not cause men to batter. Many people who live stressful lives (battered women, for example) do not batter. Moreover, men who batter and attribute this to stress do not batter strangers, neighbors, or colleagues.

Do alcohol and drug abuse cause battering? Wife abusers who drink are also known to beat their wives when sober. The majority of known alcoholics do not beat their wives, and the majority of wife abusers have not been diagnosed as alcoholics (Campbell 1986, 46). Even when drunk, assaultive men were careful to avoid making their behavior public. Wife abusers, however, may become intoxicated in order to carry out violence (Hilberman 1980, 1339). Alcohol- or drug-dependent men who abuse their partners have two problems: the chemical dependency and woman-battering. Sobriety will not eliminate the battering.

Does being a child victim of or witness to child abuse cause battering? Until recently the theory that boys who were abused or witnessed abuse grew up to abuse others seemed convincing. But this research failed to include control groups (more than 90 percent of families in the United States believe that corporal punishment of children is acceptable). Many children—boys and girls—are known to have been traumatized in this way without becoming batterers. Even brothers of batterers, who presumably witnessed the same abuse as their sibling, often do not grow up to become abusers.

Does an inability to express anger cause battering? Battering is not about anger, but about control. An abusive man chooses to lose his temper. He is already in control. His partner thinks, "If he would only express his emotions," but he already is and quite well. What is needed is less self-expression; giving vent to anger increases rather than lessens the person's angry state. "Therapists who encourage abusive people to 'vent their emotions' give them what they want: authoritative support for their explosive tirades." Such advice is "dangerous, even deadly when it is handed out to controlling and perhaps violent men" (Jones and Schecter 1992, 64).

Was she battered because she provoked the violence? To suggest that a woman provokes her abuser presumes that she has control over her husband's behavior. She does not. The abuser's sinful acts should be seen as a consequence of his decision to control his intimate partner, not as in any way caused by the woman. No matter what the woman's behavior, he still chooses to be violent.

> *Client:* I didn't make the decision. She did! She pushed me too far that time!. . .
> *Counselor:* She made you lift up your hand and hit her?
> *Client:* Well, . . . no. . . . But she pushed me too far. What was I supposed to do?
> *Counselor:* You're still saying in effect that she made you hit her because she wouldn't keep quiet. I don't buy that for a second.
> *Client:* Look, maybe I'm not saying it right, but I never decided to hit her. I just lost control. . . .
> *Counselor:* You also said earlier that you only hit her below the shoulders and you said a few sessions ago that you never hit her when the kids were around. In the past, you stopped hitting her when the police arrived. You also have never hit her in public. That sounds to me like you're making definite decisions how, where, and under what circumstances to hit her. You're very much in control.
> *Client:* Well, I can see what you're saying, but I was like a crazy man.
> *Counselor:* If you were crazy and out of control as you claim, why didn't you kill her? Why did you stop?
> *Client:* She was moaning a lot. I was afraid I'd hurt her badly.
> *Counselor:* So you made decisions—when to start, how to hit, and when to stop. You were definitely very much in control of your behavior, weren't you? (Stordeur and Stille 1989, 213–14)

While many batterers claim that their partners provoked them, no documentation exists that shows that women are more verbally aggressive than men or that men only hit when women are verbally aggressive (see Ganley

1989, 207). In fact, one study found that "physically abusive husbands were more verbally aggressive than their wives" (see Ganley 1989, 207). In addition, the woman may sense that her partner is near to attacking and may precipitate a less lethal explosion: "When the anticipatory anxiety becomes intolerable, women sometimes act to precipitate the inevitable assault" (Hilberman 1980, 1339). Furthermore, a man may be upset about his partner's verbal response to him, but this is not battering: "These men have not been assaulted by their mates and they are not terrorized by them" (Ganley 1981, 13).

A woman's behavior may aggravate or anger him. She may be intoxicated, overweight, talking back, or even be having an affair (which is rarely the case but is often assumed by an abuser); none of these behaviors on her part, however, justify his beating her. The only justification for the use of physical force is self-defense in the face of immanent threat of physical danger. A woman rarely poses a physical threat to a man unless she has a weapon.

Was she battered because she was not "Christian enough"? Sometimes a woman is told by the abuser that she deserves to be punished because she has failed to conform to Christian behavior. Generally, he means that she has not conformed to his notion of Christian *wifely* behavior. Often, he will refer to Ephesians 5 as his justification for bringing her back into line. But this justification is tied directly to his need to control her, in which scriptural injunctions dictate her behavior, but never his.

Perpetrators may have multiple problems: They may be alcoholics, veterans suffering from post-traumatic stress disorder, survivors of child abuse, or victims of racism, but these are not the reasons that they abuse someone else. Battering behavior establishes control and as a result, "for a controlling partner, there will always be something 'wrong' " (Jones and Schecter 1992, 80). The abusive man's behavior is the problem; explaining why he is abusive will not bring about any change. No matter how compelling the explanations can be, identifying an explanation will not and cannot stop the abuse. This is because abusive behavior is something that can be controlled. He exercises a great deal of self-control in other situations where he experiences stress, is drunk, carries with him his childhood scars, is a combat veteran.

Battering is learned behavior. With it the perpetrator gains his way. Because it works, battering is repeated. Indeed, because intermittent reinforcement is the strongest reinforcer of behavior, "battering only has to work some of the time to be repeated again and again" (Ganley 1989, 214).

THE EFFECTS OF BATTERING

In response to battering, the victim changes something about herself in an effort to accommodate the perpetrator. Frequently, this involves restricting her freedom, stopping relationships with friends or family he has objected to (which is usually all of her friends and family since they all pose a threat to his control), or even quitting work. Often his behavior limits her access to a car or her ability to even leave the house. Meanwhile, she attempts to soothe and please the controlling man, complying with his demands, agreeing with his opinions, denouncing his enemies. She accepts blame when things are not her fault and squelches any anger for fear of igniting his. She makes excuses for him. All to no avail. "When a woman tries to keep a partner calm by pleasing him, he gains exactly what he wants. He exercises his power over her and gets his way on a daily basis. It is ironic that she thinks she is 'managing' best when in fact she is most under his control" (Jones and Schecter 1992, 36).

Figure 1, Power and Control Wheel, identifies aspects of battering behavior and its underlying motivation as emotional power and control. As noted, a variety of coercive methods may be selected in an attempt to establish or maintain this control. Physical and sexual abuse, the outer rim, help to establish the control; once established, however, physical battering may not be needed to maintain the emotional hold. "What matters to the controller is not what he does but what he gains by doing it" (Jones and Schecter 1992, 13). A mere look from a batterer serves to control her once battering has been established in the relationship, in the same way that a parent can simply look at a child to reinforce authority.

Anne Ganley has introduced a helpful distinction between hands-on and hands-off battering. *Hands-on battering* involves physical contact with the victim's body through sexual or physical battering. *Physical battering* "includes all aggressive behavior done by the offender to the victim's body" (1981, 9) *Sexual battering* "includes physical attacks on the victim's breasts/genitals or forced sexual activity accompanied by either physical violence or the threat of physical violence" (10).

Hands-off battering, in contrast, involves psychological battering and destruction of pets or property. *Psychological battering* includes threats (such as suicide, violence against a mate or others, removing the children, or deporting foreign-born wives), forcing the victim to perform degrading acts (such as eating cigarettes left in an ashtray, licking the kitchen floor), controlling the victim's activities (such as sleeping and eating habits, social relationships, access to money), attacking the victim's self-esteem, denying the validity of her ideas and feelings, or doing things intentionally to frighten the victim, (such as driving dangerously, playing with weapons).

Effects on the Traumatized Woman

After experiencing hands-on and hands-off battering, a woman suffers a complex interplay of physical and psychological trauma. She has lost a great deal because of the battering. First, she has lost safety—and the normalcy and peace of mind that accompanies one's sense of safety. Second, she has also lost

Figure 1: Power and Control Wheel

USING INTIMIDATION
Making her afraid by using looks, actions, gestures • smashing things • destroying her property • harming pets • displaying weapons • yelling • stalking her • slamming doors • Driving recklessly • acting "crazy," invincible, or like "I have nothing to lose"

USING EMOTIONAL ABUSE
Putting her down • making her feel bad about herself • calling her names • making her think she's crazy • playing mind games • humiliating her • making her feel guilty • using things that matter to her against her • negatively comparing her to others • unreasonable demands or expectations • honeymooning her

USING ISOLATION
Controlling who she sees and talks to, what she reads, where she goes • limiting her outside involvement • using jealousy to justify actions • telling her who she should trust • interfering with her job • attacking her family • embarrassing her in front of others

USING OBFUSCATION
Denying • blaming • minimizing • withholding • omitting • externalizing • distorting • justifying • shifting responsibility • procrastinating • lying

USING OTHERS
Using the children to relay messages • using visitation to harass her • threatening to take the children away • using religion to control her • making her feel guilty about her job, her friends, her family, etc. • degrading her about her relationships • abusing the children

USING MALE PRIVILEGE
Treating her like a servant • making all the decisions • acting like the "master of the castle" • defining men's and women's roles • acting like god • deciding who is responsible for what • deciding who thinks or feels "right" • being a "know-it-all" • making all of the rules

USING ECONOMIC ABUSE
Preventing her from getting or keeping a job • making her ask for money • giving her an allowance • not letting her know about or have access to family income • controlling her money • destroying her property • wasting family income • making all financial decisions • forcing her to work to earn income

USING COERCION AND THREATS
Making and/or carrying out threats to do something to hurt her • threatening to leave her, to commit suicide, to report her to welfare • pressuring her to drop charges and/or to do illegal things • threatening negative consequences if she doesn't cooperate • pressuring her with gifts, promises, apologies

Adapted by Alternatives to Domestic Aggression, Catholic Social Services of Washtenaw County, Ypsilanti, Mich., from original by Domestic Abuse Intervention Project, 206 West Fourth Street, Duluth, MN 55806. Used by permission. On the original wheel, the type appears within the spaces between the spokes.

the ability to set boundaries and have them and her privacy respected. Third, she may lose her sense of reality as it is displaced by the abuser's sense of reality, her sense of direction as the abuser's control overwhelms it, her sense of decency and her belief in decency as it gives way to violation and being violable. Fourth, she begins to lose or loses her self-esteem, ability to trust, confidence in herself, sense that the world is just and that God is just. Fifth, she feels an increasing sense of isolation from others and may experience a diminishment of interpersonal resources. Finally, concepts and feelings such as faith, hope, charity, worth, innocence, goodness, joy, love, connectedness, intimacy, and purity are all seriously undermined.

Jones and Schecter identify five key feelings experienced by women abused by their partners:

> fear, shame, guilt, anger, and the nameless feeling of "going crazy.". . . When . . . subjected to extreme or violent control, . . . a great many women feel that they are losing control altogether and going out of their minds. Many women are troubled by insomnia or nightmares. Some have fantasies of hurting themselves or others. Some feel as though they leave their bodies—particularly if they are subjected to sexual assault—while others report the numb and "dead" condition. (1992, 42, 44)

Women suffer a wide variety of somatic reactions to the battering, such as choking sensations, gastrointestinal symptoms, and symptoms "often connected to previous sites of battering" (Hilberman 1980, 1341). They also experience paralyzing terror, agitation, distrust, violent nightmares, "anxiety bordering on panic . . . chronic apprehension of imminent doom" (1341). The trauma of marital rape can cause nausea and vomiting, soreness, bruising, muscle tension, headaches, fatigue, and injuries to the genital area. Flashbacks and haunting nightmares often linger for years.

The marital rape victim may feel strain and stress because she is constantly reminded by the presence of her rapist husband of the rape and the possibility of another attack. "Rape by intimates in general is more, not less, traumatic than rape by strangers" because the rapist continues to live with his victim (Finkelhor and Yllo 1983, 127). Moreover, women victimized by battering rapes said that these rapes were especially traumatizing because of "the more personal, intimate nature of the sexual abuse," as opposed to the sense that the "beatings seem[ed] more external" (135). Rape by a husband or lover increases the vulnerability of the victim because "the person to whom she might ordinarily turn for safety and protection [in the aftermath of a rape] is precisely the source of danger" (Herman 1992, 62–63).

Women suffering violence must be able to anticipate violence against them and attempt to prepare in advance to avoid being seriously hurt or killed. What an immense burden on them! Each woman must think about escape avenues. What windows, elevators, stairwells, or fire escapes can she use? In order to ensure quick response from the police, each woman must consider confiding in someone who is nearby. Who can befriend her? She must figure out places of safety both inside and outside of the house, as well as what rooms to avoid if there is an argument. If she has separated from the man who batters, then she has to anticipate what to do if he threatens her while she is driving home or using public transportation. She has to change the time and place where she goes grocery shopping and does her banking. She may have to move several times in attempting to escape her abuser's violence. She may lose her job because of absenteeism caused by illnesses resulting from the battering. She may lose family and friends. She may lose her church community because she has separated from her abusive husband. On top of the physical trauma of battering, constant vigilance and feelings of abandonment take a huge toll.

Rewards for the Man Who Batters

Abusive men choose when and how to be abusive. They could choose not to rape their wives anally, not to throw them down the stairs, not to threaten them verbally or emotionally. But abusive men profit from their behavior. Their partners quit jobs or take jobs, get pregnant or have abortions, cut themselves off from their friends, keep the kids quiet at times or send them away. Men who batter not only believe they have the right to use violence, but receive rewards for behaving in this manner, namely, obedience and loyalty. In addition, battering guarantees that the man wins disputes, that the status quo in the relationship is maintained, and that the woman will not leave him (Stordeur and Stille 1989, 74).

While there is no one batterer type, many perpetrators share some common characteristics. Perpetrators believe that they are entitled to have their own way at the expense of others. Their tendency is to deny (I didn't do it), minimize (it didn't cause any harm), or externalize (she caused it) their behavior. They may deny sensations of vulnerability and weakness. When they have these emotions, they look for other explanations, such as their partner made them feel uncomfortable. They translate most strong emotions, especially unpleasant ones, into anger. Avoiding emotions results in "their being slow to recognize stress or frustration, allowing it to build until they feel that their anger is out of control" (Stordeur and Stille 1989, 38–39).

They are both repelled by the strong feelings that intimacy provokes and fearful of rejection and distance. Excessively dependent on their partners, they exhibit jealousy and possessiveness. Unable to empathize with the way that their violence is experienced by others, they think only of themselves and how they are suffering. They may feel low self-esteem because they do not like their violence, but they do not know of alternatives. They may become depressed and suicidal.

Nevertheless, men who batter are deliberate in their violence: They decide where, when, under what circumstances, in what way, and at whom they will act violently. They decide whether to make wounds visible or invisible. They batter their wives or partners, not their bosses or their friends. They make such calculations because they need to be in control, and culture has provided few aversive consequences. "As violence becomes easier and easier to use, men fail to see the consequences of their behavior" (Schecter 1982, 222). Feelings of power reward men for assaulting their partners. How damaging this is to the man himself! His battering behavior results in reinforcing a distorted view of reality. As he begins to feel god-like, he may lose access to a healing and saving God.

Crises for Children

Children are affected by battering behavior against their mothers. An estimated 90 percent of the children in families with battering are aware of the battering that occurs there. Yet a terrible denial pervades the household, as though the children do not know and thus are not harmed.

Children who are aware may have witnessed beatings or rapes, thereby experiencing their mother's powerlessness and humiliation. Even though these children want to protect their mother, they usually are unable to do so and feel guilty about their inability to intervene. Many lose their childhood because their sense of security has been violated, they feel dramatically unsafe, and they are no longer innocent—they are anxious as to when the next attack will occur. Sometimes they construe themselves as the cause of the violence. They fear being abandoned, especially if they should fail to keep this violence secret. They often feel the mother's powerlessness as her fault and feel enraged with her, not the batterer. Children as young as three and four have had to assume responsibility for siblings when their mother is physically or emotionally incapacitated by the battering.

Children who are aware of the abuse need to know that they are not responsible for the behavior of their mother's partner. But their isolation and secret burden prevent them from seeking help. Isolated and frightened, they carry the burden of shame and responsibility, of guilt and anger. Children's stress-related physical reactions may include headaches, asthma, ulcers, rashes, abdominal pains, constipation, hearing, and speech problems. They may experience developmental delay or language problems. While younger children may endure impaired concentration, older boys express aggressive, disruptive behavior, and teenage girls may be withdrawn, passive, clinging, and anxious.

Batterers often inflict injuries on children as well as on their partners. Some of these injuries are nondirected, but dangerous. Children may be hurt when objects are thrown or weapons used. They may be forced to watch the killing of their pet animal. Infants may be injured if they are being held by their mothers when the batterer inflicts violence. Older children may be hurt when trying to defend or protect their mother.

Other injuries to children are directed at them. Serious abuse of children occurs most frequently in the context of woman-battering, and the fathers are usually the perpetrators (Parker et al. 1992, 2).

> Children in homes plagued by domestic violence are abused at a rate 15 times higher than the national average. Over fifty percent of wife abusers beat their children, with some studies placing the rate as high as seventy to eighty percent. As the severity of the wife abuse increases, the severity of the child abuse also increases. In addition, daughters are over six times more likely to be sexually abused in homes where wife abuse occurs. ("Developments" 1993, 1608–9)

Most parental kidnapping occurs in the context of woman-battering (Parker et al. 1992, 2). Sixty-three percent of boys from 11 to 20 years of age who are serving time for homicide killed their mother's abuser.

Battering increases the chances that a woman may batter her children. One study found that mothers were eight times more likely to hurt their children when the mothers were themselves battered than when they were safe (Walker 1984). Thus, to put this another way, "children in homes where domestic violence occurs are physically abused or seriously neglected at a rate of 1500 percent higher than the national average in the general population" (See Fortune 1991, 112).

APPROPRIATE INTERVENTION

Battering requires that caregivers respond appropriately and directly. Both the victim and the perpetrator feel pain and confusion. But their needs are different and in conflict. She lives in terror, he lives with shame. The violence must be named; protection and advocacy for the victims offered; the perpetrator held accountable; and society altered to prevent further abuse. The themes of naming the violence, providing safety for the woman, and maintaining accountability for the man are key aspects of appropriate intervention.

The Abused Woman Needs Safety

The reality of the victim's experience needs to be expressed and acknowledged, the trauma addressed and healed, and the abuser's violent acts unequivocally challenged through the force of community sanctions.

Women should react quickly after experiencing violence from their male partners. Involving someone else, especially the police, is essential. Women need to be safe. Except in extremely rare instances, achieving safety requires separation "for as long as it takes for [her] partner to stop the violence, control, and emotional abuse. This will take at least six months and possibly years" (NiCarthy 1987, 8). They will also need to establish "legal temporary custody and child support arrangements that maximize safety for [them] and the children" (8).

Each woman needs to understand that no quick solution for her partner's decision to use battering behavior is available. His decision to use such behavior is his responsibility and his alone. Often women and their counselors head in the wrong direction by asking, in effect, what the woman did to prompt such behaviors. Such questions assume that the woman has control over her husband's behavior. No matter what the woman's behavior is, he still chooses to be violent. Each battered woman needs to hear a statement such as this:

> For a controlling partner, there will always be something "wrong." A man's "reason" for exploding—or the "reason" you've come up with— has little to do with why he really explodes. That's why correcting your "mistakes" has so little effect in the long run. Although your partner acts as if you did something "wrong," he really blows up for a different reason. He needs to demonstrate that he is in control. His abusive behavior is simply a show of power over you. That's why if you correct your "mistake" today, something else will upset him tomorrow. You can't win. And *that* really is the point he is trying to demonstrate, even though he wants you to believe otherwise. (Jones and Schecter 1992, 80–81)

She needs to understand that men will continue using violence until a significant intervention is made that either controls the violent behavior or removes the victims from their control (Stordeur and Stille 1989, 152).

She also needs an interpretative framework that helps her challenge her husband's explanations and honors her perspective. A battered women's service is best equipped to provide this. They will help her see how she has actually been adjusting her worldview to his worldview, constantly accommodating conflicting information.

The usual interpretive frame latches onto symptoms such as alcoholism or emotional problems rather than on the battering behavior. But this misnames the problem and gives the batterer the "message that his nonviolence is negotiable—depending on his ability or motivation to better himself, develop insight, or improve his (or his wife's) communication skills" (D. Adams 1988, 177). The search for reasons assumes that explaining the violence will bring about a cessation of the violence. This is not the case. He controls himself in other situations and needs to be held accountable with his family.

The safety planning and accompanying counseling that battered women need can best be gotten from specialized service providers to battered women. An achievable goal for all caregivers is to mobilize community resources so that she is safe, he is held accountable, and the resources are at hand to help her survive.

The Man Who Batters Needs Accountability

Just as battering is learned, alternatives to battering can be learned, and men who batter need to acquire and choose these alternatives.

Studies, statistics, and individual testimony demonstrate clearly that the most effective way to stop violence against women is to hold the abuser accountable. In its review of developments in the law in response to domestic violence, the *Harvard Law Review* describes a coordinated community response to controlling assailants through "stringently-enforced protection orders and vigorous prosecution, combined with community education" ("Developments" 1993, 1522). In counseling sessions that are a part of such a community response, focusing on the man's decision to act in a violent manner is essential.

> *Client:* Insecurity. I guess it goes way back. . . . [*describes his experiences growing up*]. I've always been insecure with women.
> *Counselor:* This is helping me to understand why you're insecure but not why you hit your wife.
> *Client:* Sometimes I take things the wrong way . . . I overreact . . . I guess you could say, because of my insecurity. My shrink said I was like a time bomb waiting to go off . . .
> *Counselor:* A lot of people feel insecure but they are not violent. What I'm interested in finding out is how do you make the decision to hit your wife — and to break the law — even if you are feeling insecure?
> *Client:* I never really thought of it that way, as a decision. (D. Adams 1988, 176)

Aversive consequences — especially arrest, accompanied by court-mandated counseling, sometimes loss of his job, separation from his family, time in jail — demonstrate that violence does not work. They remove the rewards of battering. Four factors seem to make prosecution successful. First, criminal prosecution establishes that battering is criminal activity, not interpersonal problems gone awry. Second, probable-cause arrest policies in communities result in a decrease in incidents of violence. Third, invoking legal sanctions demonstrates accountability, whereas accountability remains an issue when sanctions are not invoked. Fourth, arrest can bring about court-mandated counseling. "Court-mandated treatment is necessary for many who batter. Due to their personality characteristics of denial, minimization, externalization, and impulsivity, many batterers will either avoid or fail to complete voluntary treatment programs" (Ganley 1981, 1). The dropout rate for voluntary treatment continues to be high (Jones and Schecter 1992, 108), but court-mandated counseling imposes a degree of accountability that allows for monitoring his commitment to change and provides consequences if he continues to inflict violence on others.

Children Need Their Own and Their Mother's Safety

Abuse of children provides another way for the abuser to maintain control over their mother. Intervention to assure the battered mother's safety and autonomy is needed, otherwise she cannot protect her children from the abusive behavior of her partner. If they have harmed the children, then they need to stop and learn alternatives to this behavior. Battered women's shelters provide a safe space for children, as well as their mothers, and offer help in acquiring positive parenting skills.

The children need stability, a sense that someone cares for them and will take care of them, and the consistent message that one does not act violently with the people one loves. Children need to know that they are not the cause of the batterer's violence. If their mother leaves the batterer, then they need to know that they are not the cause of the breakup of their mother's relationship. They need the community to affirm to their mother that a single-parent home without violence is preferable to a dual-parent home with violence.

Children not only need to be safe, they need to be physically and materially secure. If their mother separates from the batterer, however, then both material comfort and material necessity are at risk. Upon separation or divorce, women and children are almost always thrust into poverty. In addition, "batterers are significantly less likely to sign agreements for child support, and as many as 55 percent of batterers pay no child support, while only 28.3 percent may fully comply with support orders" (Parker et al. 1992, 2). Children need the community to help their mothers with housing, clothing, and food if that is what they require to stay free of the batterer's controlling behavior.

Each Needs Just Relationships

Battering is a violation of right relationships between persons: This attempt to control his intimate partner may be evidence of the perpetrator's alienation, brokenness, and estrangement. Surely such behavior causes alienation, brokenness, and estrangement in the victims. Battering destroys a relationship predicated on trust and sharing. This relationship can be healed if and only if the violence and control stop, and the victimized partner desires to continue the relationship.

Marie Fortune has identified a three-goal process for pastoral care that addresses this:

1. Protection of the victim or victims from further abuse.
2. Stopping the abuser's violence.
3. Restoration of the family relationships if possible or mourning the loss of the relationship.

These goals must be the mandates of pastors responding to battering. Fortune explains:

> The third goal of ministry with victims and abusers presents the possibility of reconciliation and healing of individuals and of relationships. But this goal is entirely dependent on the successful accomplishment of goals 1 and 2. Restoration of a relationship is impossible prior to the authentic accomplishment of these more urgent goals. (1991, 197–98).

THE CHURCH'S RESPONSE

Acknowledging that woman-battering occurs among so-called good Christian families in congregations can be difficult. Often such admission is taken as saying that the church failed. When a caregiver advises a woman to leave an abusive partner, many will take this as a sign of ineffective pastoral care or counseling. Pressure to maintain the image of the so-called happy family and congregation seems to be especially intense in African-American, Latino, Native American, and Asian-American congregations because of the nexus of family, church, and community (see White 1985, 64; Zambrano 1985, 164–66) and legitimate fear of repercussion from the dominant white community. Yet this violence is present in all social, ethnic, and religious communities; no woman is immune from danger. All around, the concern for appearance traps many ministers into giving bad advice and many women into staying with dangerous men.

Speaking the truth, then, places both ministers and battered women in a similar dilemma, namely, speaking the truth seems to betray the larger community. The difference between the denial of a battered woman and the denial of the church is that the woman (and her children) in all probability continue to suffer violence, while the minister and other church members are safely insulated from the violent truth.

First, a shift in focus is needed: The church needs to develop a proactive pastoral care response to woman-battering that emphasizes the importance of action, especially referring battered women to services for battered women, and ensuring that the justice system provides accountability to the perpetrator. Such action is based on a theological understanding. Battering is not only a violation of right relationships but also a sin against the entire Christian community because it creates a destructive environment. In addition, the community is denied the full participation of some of its members in its circle of trust. The entire community is responsible for holding the batterer accountable.

Second, naming the violence to the congregation is essential. Words need to be said to victims in the church: "You are not alone, God wants you to be safe." The perpetrators need to hear, "You are responsible for your behavior. We care enough about you to hold you responsible." The church, when such words are enacted, can become a part of the process of offering hope and the promise of healing.

Third, once violence has been introduced by an abusive man into a relationship, then all persons must work for the safety of the victims, even over keeping the family unit intact. Whenever the church fails to respond to the safety needs of the victim, then the church is abandoning its responsibility. Values about marriage's sanctity cannot overshadow values about the sanctity of the victim's life. This perspective is consistent with the biblical call to justice and mercy, and the counselor's call to heal wounded individuals.

Abuse renders the marriage relationship conditional. The abuser breaks the covenant through his behavior. The marriage was destroyed when violence was introduced into it, not when a woman acts or is encouraged to act to protect herself from the man who is harming her. Violence—not a woman's decision to leave—breaks up the family (Eilts, 1988). Divorce may save her life and his.

Fourth, many women experience their marriage covenant as binding them not only to their husband, but also to their church. When a man uses violence against his partner, she is then caught in two separate but intertwined covenants: one involving God, the woman, and her husband, and the other God, the church, the woman, and her marriage. It is the church's responsibility to release her from any perceived covenant involving the church as well as helping her understand the reality that the abuser was the one who actually broke the covenant between the couple and God.

Finally, confused values require challenge by a prophetic voice. Because of the larger community's ignorance about violence, pastoral care requires a prophetic side. Perhaps the church's concern for appearances or other causes have created an incredible inertia within the church to respond appropriately to the problem of woman-battering. Pastoral care must stake itself clearly on the fault line between appearances and reality, between abusers and victims, between silence and prophecy, between ongoing violence and its cessation. Ministers must begin to enunciate clearly that the stigma is on the community, including the church community, that fails to stop the violence, not on the woman who seeks from clergy and her church community help in stopping the violence.

1

NAMING

In order to be of assistance either to a woman being abused by her partner or to the man who is hurting her, ministers need to state clearly that they are aware that abuse is occurring. Ministers may think that they have indicated a willingness to help those who are abused or abusers; but often such hints of concern are so veiled that they are not experienced as signs of help. Likewise, the victim or the perpetrator may think that the abuse has been disclosed, but because it may have been done in such an indirect way, or so timidly, the minister did not hear it as a disclosure about violence. Ministers may think that they did their best to reach out, while the victims and perpetrators may think that when they told, the minister was unresponsive.

One can imagine many instances when shouting for help would be appropriate, for instance, when mugged on the street. But when is the appropriate time for the woman who is being battered to shout for help? After all, a stranger does not threaten her; the man she loves does. He is not violent all the time; the memory of special moments—and his own current behavior, which at times may be less threatening—work to distort her sense of danger. He is threatening, but he has promised to stop; he is violent, but he needs her so badly. Moreover, the man she loves has slowly reconstructed her world, depriving her of outside contacts, perhaps destroying symbols of those contacts (like photographs), monitoring her movements and telephone conversations. At which moment in this insidiously shrinking circle of opportunities will she speak of the unspeakable?

THE POWER OF NAMING

Paulo Freire observes that "To exist, humanly, is to *name* the world, to change it" (1972, 61). The power of naming is the power of self-authorization. Ministers must offer both victims and abusers this power because each may minimize the violence, reinterpret what occurred, excuse the battering behavior. She must name her world—including his battering behavior—so that she can be safe; he must name his world—including his battering behavior—as the first step in stopping it. Silence protects the status quo, and the status quo favors men who batter.

28

The care provider must create the climate for moving from silence to naming the violence, thus offering an invitation to healing and liberation. When ministers name by speaking about battering and abusive behavior within a church context, they offer an invitation in two important ways. First, denial of responsibility for the violence and terror of abusive behavior is a common character trait of the abuser. The abuser must be encouraged to name his abusive behavior. Unless he does that he will not avail himself of help, for he believes he does not have a problem; she does. Second, denial of the seriousness or the meaning of the violence and the terror is a survival mechanism for the victim. In fact, she may not have a name for what she is experiencing. To offer the name then is to offer the possibility of change.

WHY NAMING DOES NOT OCCUR

Many reasons can be offered to explain why naming does not occur. Shame is associated with woman-battering—for both victim and abuser. Secrets are hard to give up. Telling is hard. Thus the minister often needs to explore these reasons with the congregation in various settings in order to encourage the naming process.

Typical Inhibitors for Battered Women

In cases of woman-battering, telling is suffused with feelings of stigma, fear, defilement, guilt, and denial. Disclosing abuse is scary. It's embarrassing. She feels responsible and may fear being prejudged. Naming may not occur because she is suffering from the shock and stress of ongoing traumatization. Humiliated by the abuse and ashamed of her powerlessness in stopping it, her shameful feelings multiply when she becomes further ashamed of her silence. Seeing herself as being dishonest, she may become more isolated and withdrawn or so embarrassed that she does not tell anyone what has happened.

Telling on someone who has power over her increases the fear that people will not believe her or understand her. She may see herself as disloyal if she tells. She may fear reprisal, that she will be punished for telling, or that he will hurt or take the kids. She may wish to spare him embarrassment. She may fear repercussions from authorities: deportation or the removal of her children. She may remind herself that she was brought up not to tell on family. She may feel sorry for the man who harms her. She may believe that she should turn the other cheek.

The victim may fear not only the reaction of the abuser but also the reaction of the care provider: disbelief, judgment, ostracism, or worse, an inadequate or insensitive response such as believing that she likes the abuse. Her batterer has probably threatened, "No one will ever believe you if you tell on me." She may fear that the counselor cannot make sense of what she discloses, instead being stunned by her shocking information. She may have assessed her minister, sensing an inability to hear the information. After experiencing constant criticism by her partner, turning to someone else for help means opening herself up to others' criticisms. She may fear that others will confirm her own harsh self-judgment.

The woman may have been raped by her husband but does not name her experience of forced sex as rape. Not having a name to give this experience means that she cannot talk about it with anybody.

The gender of the minister may be a barrier to telling. A woman may not feel safe telling a man. Many women who suffer violence may fear that clergymen will identify with their partner, not with them, and dismiss the seriousness of his behavior through identification with his good characteristics — that he is wonderful, he has done so much good, and so forth, that his behavior was an aberration, not a practice, not an ongoing problem. Many marital rape victims experience the long-term effect of not being able to trust men. What they need is the opportunity of talking with their peers — other women victimized by assaultive partners.

The victim may not tell because she sees the minister as naive and able to be manipulated by the batterer. Concerned that the man who hurts her will use counseling as a form of control, she sees no point in bringing in a care provider whom she thinks would allow rather than stop the manipulation, thus sanctioning the abuse.

She may not tell because she believes that God would not give her anything that she could not bear. She may fear that the minister will uphold the sanctity of the marriage covenant over her abuse.

She may not name the violence because she denies that battering is occurring. She uses make-up and sunglasses to hide bruises and wounds. She appears at an emergency room saying she fell down the stairs.

She may admit that she is being battered, but she denies that battering is a problem. Facing the reality of her situation may be too frightening. It is especially difficult for a wife to admit that her husband raped her because that would mean that she is living with a rapist and that she is always vulnerable to rape.

In naming the controlling behavior that she has suffered, she faces the burden of reporting the negative naming that she may have experienced. As a part of his psychological battering of her, her partner may have called her cunt, bitch, stupid, slave, dummy, whore. If she is a woman of color, this demeaning language may be racialized as well (a *Black* cunt, an *Asian* slave). These words, an influential part of her abuse, may be too painful to repeat and may communicate multiple oppressions too overwhelming to confront.

Naming the abuse may not occur because she does not know anything is wrong. She may believe that violence is normal. She may not know that it is against the law to rape or batter women. Naming may not occur because although she knows that something is wrong, when she told someone, the person never responded. Or, knowing something was terribly wrong, she told and the controlling man retaliated. She may think that everyone, including the minister, knows, but nobody, including the minister, cares.

She may not name the violence because she, like the man who batters, minimizes what he is doing. She minimizes his behavior because she fears and loves him. She may rationalize the violence by explaining to herself her partner is not responsible because he is sick, alcoholic, unemployed, a veteran, a victim himself, or under stress—focusing on his characteristics rather than his behavior.

She may believe that she acted provocatively or that she has been unchristian and this results in her battering. Or, she may believe that she controls the violence by accommodating her husband's various demands.

She may fear that telling will mean that she has to leave, and she may not be ready to make this decision. David Finkelhor and Kersti Yllo observe: She avoids "facing the realities of an intolerable marriage because the alternatives—loneliness, loss of financial security, admission of failure—are so frightening" (1983, 121).

Naming may be occurring without explicit naming. In physical symptoms that she identifies, in emotional issues that she brings to a minister such as depression and anxiety, in theological issues that are her concern, such as a loss of faith, a feeling of God's abandonment, being in a spiritual war, or anger at God—in all these ways she may be saying that she is suffering abuse.

Naming may not occur for many because they have no name to give to their experience. But when, through representation and identification, an image is offered by the media, naming pours forth. For instance, after the arrest of O.J. Simpson for the murder of his ex-wife and her friend, and the subsequent publicity about woman-battering, women responded by inundating shelters and hotlines for battered women with calls. Suddenly naming is possible because the media has represented their own experience. Similarly, after a clergyperson mentions battering during worship, women abused by their partners will be more likely to approach her or him and discuss their own beatings.

Being an Adult Survivor of Child Sexual Abuse

According to Judith Herman, the adult survivor of child sexual abuse is "at great risk of repeated victimization in adult life. The data on this point are compelling, at least with respect to women. The risk of rape, sexual harassment, or battering, though high for all women, is approximately doubled for survivors of childhood sexual abuse" (1992, 111). Implicitly answering the Is she masochistic? question, Herman explains this compounding of trauma:

> The survivor's intimate relationships are driven by the hunger for protection and care and are haunted by the fear of abandonment or exploitation. In a quest

for rescue, she may seek out powerful authority figures who seem to offer the promise of a special caretaking relationship. . . .

Almost inevitably, the survivor has great difficulty protecting herself in the context of intimate relationships. Her desperate longing for nurturance and care makes it difficult to establish safe and appropriate boundaries with others. Her tendency to denigrate herself and to idealize those to whom she becomes attached further clouds her judgment. Her empathic attunement to the wishes of others and her automatic, often unconscious habits of obedience also make her vulnerable to anyone in a position of power or authority. Her dissociative defensive style makes it difficult for her to form conscious and accurate assessments of danger. . . .

Repeated abuse is not actively sought but rather is passively experienced as a dreaded but unavoidable fate and is accepted as the inevitable price of relationship. Many survivors have such profound deficiencies in self-protection that they can barely imagine themselves in a position of agency or choice. The idea of saying no to the emotional demands of a parent, spouse, lover, or authority figure may be practically inconceivable. . . . A well-learned dissociative coping style also leads survivors to ignore or minimize social cues that would ordinarily alert them to danger. (111–12)

This "sensitivity to the aggressor" as Ellyn Kaschak calls it (1992, 126) is one of the reasons that a survivor of child sexual abuse can benefit greatly from the support a battered women's program can provide her; from her peers she can gain valuable insight into self-care, assessing danger, and establishing boundaries. Besides having all the needs from being a woman harmed by her partner, she also needs a space to explore what happened to her as a child. These are two different needs. She needs to be alerted to support groups for survivors of child sexual abuse and assured that the issues arising from her sexual exploitation as a child can be addressed in a safe place through a specialized program.

The Race of the Victim and Her Abuser

Women—young and old; Hispanic, Asian-American, African-American, Native American, and white; able-bodied and with disabilities; citizens and documented or undocumented immigrants—are all victimized by violent partners. But the cultural context in which they live will influence with whom they share their victimization.

Racism has inhibited the development of resources for survivors who are women of color. Stereotypes may impede service delivery, too. An example of this is when a white medical professional attributed a Hispanic woman's problems to craziness, discounting the evidence that a pastor held in her hands—X rays that showed three broken ribs from being pushed down the stairs. To this pastor, it was clear that racism impeded service delivery.

Because justice in our country is not color-blind, because women of color face obstacles in being believed, because assailants of women of color are less likely to be prosecuted than assailants of white women (see Crenshaw 1992), women of color may not view the criminal justice system as a source of help for them. Specifically, African-American women may be aware of unjustified police violence against African-American men. Moreover, the emphasis on the family in African-American communities adds extraordinary pressure on women hurt by their partners: "Black women have been conditioned to repair the damage that has been done to black families because we feel it is our responsibility to keep the family together at all costs" (White 1985, 25). To African-American women, ministers can say:

> Physical and emotional abuse are not acceptable demonstrations of black manhood, even though your partner, family or friends may try to make excuses for his behavior. Black men will *not* heal their wounded pride or regain a sense of dignity by abusing black women. It is important for you to hold your partner accountable for every injury he inflicts. By doing so you stop contributing to your own pain as well as to his self-destructiveness. . . .
>
> Saying to the abusive behavior of your partner "No," does not mean you want to emasculate him, but that you believe you have a right to a loving relationship. (White 1985, 26)

Several factors influence whether Latinas will feel comfortable with naming the abuse. Bilingual resources may be necessary. Their economic situation may limit options: Because of racial discrimination, "Latinas are more concentrated in low paying, semi-skilled occupations than the overall work force" (Zambrano 1985, 131). While Latina women may be from Mexico, Central America, South America, the Dominican Republic, Puerto Rico, or Cuba, several cultural traditions exist that may influence their silence:

- Problems are usually kept in the home.
- The authority and dignity of the family are respected.
- Latinas are not accustomed to revealing their feelings to outsiders.
- Latinas have been socialized to uphold the status quo.
- Latinas often accept their destiny with resignation, accepting their family life as being the way God wants them to live. (excerpted from Zambrano, 227)

Southeast Asian and South Asian women may be discomforted with naming not because they hold any hope for change in the relationship, but because of community pressure. They know that they will lose face before their community if they leave. They need help in gathering proof of the abuse, so that they can leave with the support or at least without the condemnation of the community. The church can model this support. Moreover, bilingual resources are often necessary for serving Asian women, too.

Citizen Status

Immigrant women face additional burdens:

> The disruption and trauma of immigration—leaving one's home land and traveling to the United States—and the processes of adjustment and acculturation once here increase vulnerability in general, including vulnerability to violence in relationship. Their life after arrival may be one of poverty and extreme stress. . . . If they have fled war-torn or oppressive countries, the trauma of earlier experiences adds to their vulnerability. For example, they may fear calling on law enforcement for help, or fear talking to others because of past fear of informers. (Levy 1990, 6)

Their isolation may be aggravated by their lack of familiarity with the language, culture, legal, or social systems in this country. The batterer may use the threat of deportation, saying he will call the Immigration and Naturalization Services. This threat effectively maintains control by keeping the woman from leaving. The man who batters may have destroyed her documentation. If she is undocumented, her susceptibility to coercion increases. Precluded from most public benefits and not having the authorization to be employed, she is not able to establish economic independence. "For an undocumented battered woman, deportation could mean leaving her American-born children in the United States with their father. This situation is often a woman's foremost concern" (Family Violence Prevention Fund 1992).

The Age of the Victim

Is she young? She may sense that she faces strong disbelief about the life-threatening nature of the battering behavior because her problem is dismissed as a kid's problem. But thirteen-year-old females have been killed by their boyfriends, even after they reported violent behavior to the police. Because adolescent problems are not granted the sort of legitimacy that many adult problems are, the life-threatening nature is minimized (see Levy 1990). Holding the young assaultive man accountable through the criminal justice system becomes all the more important when one considers the absolute powerlessness of the young victim. Again, battered women's programs provide a leverage for doing this.

The Geographical Area in which the Victim Lives

Does she live in a rural area? If she does, she may face a community with fewer resources and more rigid notions about intervention in the family. Although each region is distinctive, a few common themes need to be acknowledged:

- Rural residents perceive life in their environment as healthy compared to city living and challenging this myth of bucolic rural life feels frightening.
- County sheriffs, state police, town police, and village police are often without centralized coordination in a rural area. Police scanners in individual homes make women hesitant to call upon law enforcement for help.
- Rural victims of battering face isolation imposed by distance and lack of transportation. A long-distance call is documented on the phone bill and available for an abuser's scrutiny. To enter a shelter, a woman may have to go to the nearest urban center. Not only may this be frightening because of intense fear of urban areas, but the noises and stresses of urban life may feel unbearable. NOTE: Safe home networks may be available in rural areas and are positive responses to some of these needs. (See Adams and Engle-Rowbottom 1991.)

A Lesbian Partner as Abuser

If a woman is being battered by a female partner, then she faces other forces that may militate against naming: Her partner may threaten to *out* her, that is, to expose her lifestyle to the community if she seeks help to stop the battering. She may fear seeking help because disclosing battering may reinforce others' homophobic stereotypes. She may assume that no one will believe her because she is a lesbian. Verbal abuse by her partner may have derived from homophobic stereotypes. She may believe that she deserves to be battered because she is a lesbian. She may confuse her victimization by a batterer with mutual fighting (see Lobel 1986). (Urban areas may also have anti-battering resources for gay men about which ministers need to be aware.)

Why Batterers Do Not Name Their Behavior

Disclosure is scary for the man who batters as well, although the violent results of telling are not consequences he suffers but ones that he imposes on another. Because many batterers *externalize* their behavior—seeing the cause outside one's self—disclosure may force a batterer to look more closely at his own responsibility. This he does not want to do.

Men who batter may not see their battering behavior as a problem, "or if they see it as a problem, they may not assume the responsibility for changing it" (Ganley 1991, 221). The man who batters may think that he has no other way to respond and be frightened by the idea of any change. He too may fear the minister's judgment, ostracism, disbelief. He may fear that with disclosure he will lose the relationship that is so important to him. He may also fear arrest, imprisonment, being stigmatized by the congregation, or the loss of his job. He may view women so condescendingly that he does not respect a woman minister and so could not imagine going to her for help.

This continuous pressure to deny what is going on results in story telling. Both the man who batters and his victim come to believe that he is violent either because of something she did or because of something beyond his control. This story keeps them from the truth: He batters because no one, not even he, stops him. His behavior is his responsibility. The purpose of naming, and of pastoral intervention, is to help both the man who batters and his victim to move from story telling to truth telling.

Naming involves recognizing the specific social situation of the woman. Although her community may pressure her to maintain the status quo by keeping silent, it also contains within it strengths that may be leveraged once sensitive naming has occurred. Immense barriers exist to telling. Yet a relief often emerges in breaking the silence and bringing the abuse into the open, in moving from denial to naming.

INVITING NAMING

Ministers can help break the power of the secret by naming battering, abuse, and rape as concerns of the church. This naming of abuse and battering offers a validation of the victim's reality. As in the wake of the arrest of O.J. Simpson, what was previously unspeakable, and thus in some ways unknowable, becomes nameable and thus knowable. Naming offers an alternative reality to that which has been accepted as normative, the abuser's reality.

Naming requires speaking true words about the dangers of battering; misnaming, in contrast, will minimize the life-threatening nature of battering as a spat, a family fight, a crime of passion, just an argument. He did not just "lose control"; this is not "family violence" (a term which implies a free-for-all). Naming requires accurately identifying woman abuse as woman-battering when it happens.

Ministers have several avenues available for placing the issue of woman-battering before the congregation and thus before those who are victims or abusers. They can preach that violence is not appropriate in intimate relationships and that the church stands ready to help families stop abuse. Ministers can encourage the development of a congregational position paper on violence, with involvement from all sectors of the congregation. Remarks about battering can be inserted into a sermon, the weekly or monthly letter to the congregation, in a prayer, in an article for the local newspaper. The minister can say:

I have been learning startling information. According to statistics there are at least four million women being battered by their male partners in this country. The church must be a place that says this violence must stop and that invites both abused and abusers to come forward.

Raising the issue in congregational contexts should include education efforts. Encourage adult forums, invite local resource people. Purchase multiple copies of *Keeping the Faith: Questions and Answers for the Abused Woman* (Fortune 1987) and at least one copy of *When Loves Goes Wrong: What to Do When You Can't Do Anything Right* (Jones and Schecter 1992) and *Getting Free: A Handbook for Women in Abusive Relationships* (NiCarthy 1982) for the church library. When these arrive, ensure that the women's association of the church is notified that these resources are available; the church newsletter should also announce that the church library has acquired them. Construct a sermon that responds to one of the biblical stories of violence against a woman such as 2 Samuel 13 or Judges 19 (see Trible 1984 for helpful exegesis and Newsom and Ringe 1992 for insights into these and other passages). These passages are often rendered invisible by their absence from the lectionary of mainstream denominations. Yet they provide opportunities to name and condemn violence that harms women, to reflect theologically on the issue of naming and silence, and to situate the minister as one who is willing and able to respond to this issue.

Other sermon opportunities will occur in response to the secular calendar. Discuss battering in a sermon during October, which is Domestic Violence Awareness Month. A sermon can respond to a situation in the community: increased prosecution, the establishment of a new service, or a tragedy such as a wife being murdered by her husband. Responding to any or all of these will begin to open up the naming process.

Many communities nationwide have community-based domestic violence task forces. Representation on these task forces would be a valuable way of staying apprised of community efforts to stop domestic violence. Ministers could report to their congregations what the task force is doing and invite shelter staff to present informational programs at church functions. These can also send strong messages to both the community and the church about being committed to stop violence. They may also encourage self-referrals or referrals by peers to the shelter staff.

When clergy become better informed about the issues of sexual and domestic violence and then announce in some way that they are concerned about the existence of such issues and know that these issues touch members in their congregations, they are usually shocked by the number of individuals who then approach asking for help. It is not that an epidemic has just broken out, but that by forthrightly naming the problem the clergy announce that they wish to provide healing to the wounds caused by abuse and imply that they know what to do. Thus they are seen as a resource.

CREATING THE CLIMATE FOR DISCLOSURE

To invite naming, ministers need to create the feeling that telling can happen and that by telling the battered woman is not less safe than she was before telling. In other words, ministers must create both a climate of safety and the environment for disclosure. This involves knowing and respecting boundaries while providing a sense of connection.

Climate of Safety

Remember that through the controlling behavior of her partner, the woman has learned that she has no safe space in which to express initiative. The man who batters does not allow for trial and error. Her available choices have been constricted, and her ability to choose has been destroyed: "To the chronically traumatized person, any action has potentially dire consequences" (Herman 1992, 91).

In order for a battered woman to speak the truth about her situation, she must feel safe, having a sense that her truth telling will be treated with confidentiality and that she has the latitude to speak and act without being punished. She needs to know that the counseling session cannot be overheard by a passerby or by another staff member. Broaching questions to her in a public place with people milling around is not appropriate. Keeping the door wide open in a way that conveys an invitation to others to enter while meeting with her is also inappropriate.

While the primary concern is her safety, and assuring her of the confidentiality of the discussion, she must be told that ministers are ethically if not legally mandated to report child abuse. Offer to reflect with her about the best way to do such reporting if child abuse is occurring in the home.

A climate of safety involves active listening, as well as expressing respect for her courage and acknowledging her suffering. She needs to sense that the minister will affirm rather than reprimand her for speaking. Let her know that no one ever deserves to be hit or hurt, except in cases of self-defense. Time is needed to discuss various services, such as battered women's programs, and referrals with these services are essential. Her disclosure should bring about a practical connection that helps her strategize about safety. This will confirm the benefits of telling. Providing practical information reinforces the assertion that no one deserves to be hit or hurt, indicating that such statements are not mere platitudes.

Environment for Disclosure

The counseling environment created must convey hospitality and acceptance. Ensuring sufficient time and safe space for a discussion is essential. The woman needs to feel comfortable in the minister's presence and in the physical space in which they talk. Responses need to be sensitive, nonjudgmental, and ones that do not belittle her reality. Compassion and concern are forms of invitation. Let her tell her story.

Having a clock within her eyesight helps her know what time it is, because men who batter often keep a close watch over their partner's activities and whereabouts. The minister can assure her, There is as much time as you need, don't feel rushed. But she needs to be reassured that she does not need to tell anything that she does not feel comfortable discussing. At times, if she pauses, struggling for words, the minister can say in a supportive way, Take your time.

The story, having never, or rarely, been told before, may not be coherently shaped. There may be some hesitancy or embarrassment because of this. Keep a tissue box unobtrusively near the care seeker's chair. Acknowledge her courage. Offer supportive comments, such as, I am sorry this has happened. Do not say, I know how you feel.

ASKING THE QUESTION

Many ministers assume that providing the opportunity for naming is sufficient for inviting the victim of abuse to speak up about her experience. Sending out clues that the minister cares about the issue and wants to help is not enough to prompt disclosure. Stopping short of asking her directly about her situation risks story telling because such signals are inadequate. Numerous presumptions on the part of the woman suffering violence enforce her silence so that the minister must facilitate the naming by speaking explicitly and by being willing to talk about abuse, controlling behavior, and terror. Women may come to see a minister and identify the main issue as alcoholism, their husband's financial irresponsibility, his promiscuity, their own depression, suicidal behavior, self-mutilation, worry, stress, unresolved anger, a sense of hopelessness, a faith crisis, or other concerns. The cause of these presenting problems, however, is her suffering of violence. Pastoral care that cannot identify this underlying cause fails to be pastoral.

Knowing the Signs of Abuse

One aspect of inviting naming is being alert to the signs of abuse. (See Table 1, Signs of Abuse.) Perhaps a woman who formerly was involved in the church has withdrawn from many social activities that had previously been important to her, perhaps when she is at church she is always accompanied by

---

Table 1: Signs of Abuse

• Do you see or hear about repeated bruises, broken bones, or other injuries, the result of "falls" or "accidents"?
• Does she seem frightened, withdrawn, isolated, unusually quiet, reluctant to speak?
• Do you feel uncomfortable when her partner is present? Does he criticize her in front of you, or make "joking" remarks that belittle her? Does he tell her what to do and not to do? Does she seem significantly different—perhaps unusually cheery or exceptionally quiet? Does he appear charming and solicitous while she is withdrawn, quiet, and tense?
• Are you afraid of her partner?
• Does she refer to his bad moods, anger, temper, or short fuse? Does she refer to obnoxious things he does when he drinks? Does she hint that there is trouble or conflict at home?
• Does he ignore the children or abuse them emotionally, physically, or sexually? Do they seem timid, frightened, or angelic in his presence? Do the children abuse her, verbally or physically?
• Have there been suicide or homicide attempts or threats in this family?
• Is he accusing her of having affairs with other men or women? Does he try to control her every move?
• Has there been a suspicious injury or death of a pet reported?
• Does she seem continually to try to keep things smooth, to avoid upsetting him?
• In warm weather, does she sometimes wear inappropriate clothes with long sleeves, turtlenecks, or neck scarves? (This list is excerpted and adapted from Jones and Schecter 1992, 300–301.)

---

her husband who never allows her out of his sight. Perhaps during a pastoral visit at her home she is extremely anxious. Perhaps a woman in the hospital explains her injuries nervously. College women may be battered by their boyfriends and exhibit some of the same signs of abuse as enumerated above. By knowing the signs of abuse, the minister can respond effectively to them, rather than ignoring them.

If there are signs of abuse, then find an opportunity to speak alone with the possible victim, while protecting her safety. For example, if she has stopped coming to church and the minister recognizes several signs of abuse, then a phone call is appropriate. Ensure that it is at a time when in all probability the husband is not there. If the husband comes home, then the call can be ascribed to any one of several church-related reasons.

If the minister is approached about doing regular marital counseling, then an assessment of the issues should occur through separate meetings with the husband and wife. Some of the questions listed below may be raised.

Ministers need to be able and ready to ask questions that provide an opportunity for the woman to speak the truth about her situation. Asking questions that allow for disclosure does not mean asking questions that sound like accusations, such as questions that focus on her own background (What was your family life like?) or that focus on her actions (What did you do?).

Begin with the obvious: " 'You seem so unhappy. Do you want to talk about it? I'd like to listen, and I'll keep it between us.' Even if she rejects the offer, your observation about her unhappiness supports her by affirming some of her feelings. And you have offered an open-ended opportunity for a confidential conversation in the future" (Jones and Schecter 1992, 307).

But such a general question may not prompt disclosure. Do not instead use more specific terms, such as *violence* or *abuse* because his controlling behavior may not have been defined as violence or his abuse may have been so successful that physical violence is no longer required for continued control.

Behavior, Not Characteristics

Behaviorally based descriptions are required. Jones and Schecter suggest a series of questions that focus on her experiences. They move from the general to the specific, from being expansive to becoming more direct:

1. What's it like at home for you?
2. What happens when you and your partner disagree or argue?
3. How does your partner handle things when he doesn't get his way? What does he do?
4. Are you ever scared of him? Does he threaten you?
5. Does he ever prevent you from doing things you want to do?
6. Does he ever follow you?
7. Do you have to account to him for your time?
8. Is he jealous, hard to please, irritable, demanding, critical?
9. Does he put you down, call you names, yell at you, punish you in any way?
10. Does he ever push you around or hit you?
11. Does he ever make you have sex? Does he ever make you do sexual things that you don't like? (1992, 307–8).

These questions maintain a focus on behavior rather than individual characteristics. As Jones and Schecter point out, "Notice that these questions do *not* imply that you are psychoanalyzing her, looking for explanations of her behavior, challenging her, or passing judgment. Instead, they invite the woman to talk about what the controlling partner *does* and what she *feels* about it" (307).

Knowing the Signs of an Abuser

In counseling men, ministers can also look for signs, this time signs of battering behavior. (See Table 2, Signs of an Abuser.) Anne Ganley suggests the following questions:

- How do you show anger?
- How do other family members express anger to you?
- Describe fighting behavior.

Table 2: Signs of an Abuser

- Does he think women are inferior to men? Does he frequently mention this perceived inferiority?
- Does he believe that women should be "submissive," "quiet," "dependent," "respectful," or "know their place"?
- Does he have a problem with alcohol or drugs?
- Has he ever humiliated her for her opinions about his alcohol or drug use?
- Is he constantly critical of her? Does he belittle everything she says and does?
- Does he say negative things about her friends or family?
- Does he demean her hopes? Dreams? Aspirations? Ambitions?
- Does he "love her so much" that he cannot bear for her to be in the company of anyone else?
- Is he so jealous that he becomes suspicious of her every action?
- Is he so possessive that he wants to dictate her every move?
- Does she have to ask his permission before doing even ordinary things?
- Does he fly into a rage for no apparent reason?
- Does he warn her that he is going to beat her? Verbal warnings about abuse should never be ignored.
- Does he believe that a man has the right to physically discipline or punish his partner?
- Has he ever destroyed property (her favorite china) or injured or killed their pet?
- Does he believe that God made man superior to woman and thereby gave him the privilege of beating her?
- Does he deal with stress through outbursts of violent behavior such as swearing, throwing things, breaking windows, kicking doors? (excerpted and adapted from Statman 1990, 31–37)

If he responds by saying, "Sometimes to show anger, I . . . ," the minister can respond by asking, "What do you do *other* times?" (Ganley 1981, 44). Edward Gondolf and Ellen Fisher suggest questions such as,

- Have you ever thrown objects or broken things when you are angry?
- Do you demand a strict account of how your wife manages her money?

They observe: "While a man might deny being a batterer, he may admit to occasional abusive acts which, when taken overall, amount to extreme abuse" (1988, 103).

THE DYNAMICS OF NAMING

With the breaking of the secret, anxiety over the disclosure may be acute. Assure her that anxiety when seeking help is normal. Having invited naming, do not doubt or disbelieve. The person needs to be believed. Any disbelief can be extremely damaging (Randall 1990, 939), especially because the reporter has most likely minimized the actual behavior. She needs to be believed and supported. She needs to know that she has support from the institution, the church, not just individual support and advocacy.

The movement from silence to naming is painful; while she has actually lost safety, trust, and a sense of her inviolable self, to name these losses means that she must confront other losses. In specific, she must face the loss of the idealized, romanticized relationship she thought she would have with her partner; what she most wanted she does not have. To realize that she has lost what she never had is an extremely painful realization.

From Story Telling to Truth Telling

In moving from silence to naming, one begins to confront the story that had been constructed to explain the abuse. This story generally focused on her characteristics and behavior rather than his behavior. Story telling occurs in response to confusion about why she is being hurt.

The problem with story telling is that it is most frequently a story about the woman (I did something wrong, God is punishing me, I provoked the beating). With story telling the explanations that form the narrative may change, but they always deflect the focus from the behavior of the man who batters. The truth that needs to be named is that battering is a decision the man who batters makes. By establishing control through battering, his world and his reality prevail.

The movement from story telling to truth telling occurs through the movement from the focus on the victim as the precipitant to the focus on the abuser as the one responsible for his behavior. Whereas story telling revolves around what she did wrong and how she can fix it, truth telling focuses on what he gains from his behavior. To face the sad truth of battering—that it is his responsibility, that he benefits through establishing control by battering—means losing the sense that she can do something about it. But this movement from story telling to truth telling may also be a source of liberation.

The movement from denial to naming thus initiates the movement from story telling to truth telling. Naming begins the process of recognizing that the battered woman has little control over the behavior of the man who batters. When she clings to the story that focuses on herself, she is enabled to hold to an interpretation that implies that she has some control over her situation and that she can change things. By naming the trauma in an empathetic atmosphere, she is enabled to discover the distressing truth: She cannot change her partner. This truth is frightening.

Naming as Empowering

The truth may also be liberating especially for women victimized by forced sex. Naming her coerced sexual experience may help her stop blaming herself, or feeling guilty for what has happened.

Another benefit of naming the violence is gained when such naming is affirmed by the stories of other victims of violence. Using the Power and Control Wheel, found on p. 18, and offering information on power-control tactics of abusers helps to break down the victim's isolation and place the problem of battering in its social and political context. One of the most empowering events occurs in shelters and support groups through such contextualization. By this collective naming, other battered women and battered women's advocates remove the burden of the problem from the victim.

The movement from story telling to truth telling is an important one for the man who batters as well. Dick Bathrick, of Men Stopping Violence, observes that

> it requires a lot of energy for a man to deny and minimize what he's done while at the same time holding at bay some degree of guilt and shame. The guilt and shame, especially the shame, paralyze him in his efforts to do something about his violence. When a man is confronted with the truth of his violence—while in one moment it is terrible and frightening because there's a lot of unknowns to what the consequences might be—there is also some relief that now it's no longer his own secret. (Conversation, December 1993)

Naming thus offers the beginning of the possibility for him to stop the violence, make it safe emotionally and physically for others, and to provide restitution, to restore what he's taken from her. Bathrick concludes, "Just sitting and feeling guilty and hiding it—all of those responses lead to nothing. But when a man (not all men, but some men) is confronted and then told that he needs to do something about it then things may begin to happen." He cautions, however, that some men feel no remorse and so feel no relief from naming. (Conversation, December 1993)

AFFIRMING THE POWER OF NAMING

When ministers name abuse, battering, and rape, and provide an opportunity for victims and abusers to name their experiences, they offer connection and the hope that indeed change can occur. Telling one's experience in a receptive atmosphere can feel like a prayer—or an answer to a prayer. Freire observes, "To speak a true word is to transform the world" (1990, 60). Breaking the silence about abuse offers the opportunity for victims to transform their constricted and wounding world delimited by their controlling partner or, for abusers, by their own refusal to stop controlling behaviors.

Once naming has occurred, that naming and accompanying care seeking must be put in a positive perspective. Ministers can say:

> Speaking about your experience of being hurt by your partner is not a betrayal of your relationship. The relationship was betrayed when he chose to hurt you. Speaking about it is an affirmation of your relationship with God. This naming offers reconnection, reconnecting you with a saving God, a God who is in the past and future, not just a static and dangerous present. Seeking help indicates your good judgment and strength under traumatic circumstances.

Similarly, ministers can affirm naming by the man who batters:

> Speaking about your abuse of your wife is an affirmation of your relationship with God. This naming offers reconnection, reconnecting you with a saving God, and reconnecting yourself with behavior that treats your partner as an equal and worthy of dignity. There is much work to be done. The battering must stop. But now that you have named the behavior, the work can begin. It won't be easy but God will be with you in this work.

Calling upon Freire's insights again, we must acknowledge that "no one can say a true word alone—nor can she or he say it *for* another, in a prescriptive act which robs others of their words" (1972, 61). The church community committed to stopping violence invites the saying of a true word, not alone, but in a supportive presence. Not exploiting a situation in pursuing the questions, Have you been abused? or Are you abusing someone? but inviting an expanded relationship with the outer world. By facilitating naming, we provide connection, we offer hope, we promise that change can occur.

2

BEING PREPARED

One Saturday evening, the hotline phone rang and I answered it. The woman on the other end of the telephone said to me: "My husband just held a gun to my head and said he was going to kill me. He pulled the trigger. But the gun was empty." She paused and then bravely asked her question: "Should I be worried?"

When I relate this to students in my seminary course, their initial reaction is often laughter. The first time this occurred I was startled by it. I recalled the earnestness and sincerity with which she asked the question and knew as well that the following day when she was safely sheltered with another family somewhere in the community, her husband placed a loaded gun in his car and drove up and down the streets looking in each driveway for her car. But to the students her question is infused with absurdity. They are astonished that someone must ask if this behavior is something to worry about. Her tentativeness struck them as incongruous.

In hearing victims or abusers, laughter will not be the most frequent spontaneous response that ministers must monitor; it is their reactions such as anger, shock, aversion, judgment, disbelief, or fear that may well stigmatize them to a care seeker. Preparation involves being ready and able to hear a woman say that she was harmed by her male partner and knowing how to respond.

Three skills or abilities are essential when victims disclose their experiences: processing information about the dehumanizing violence enacted by one person against another; providing practical assistance; and reflecting theologically. IMPORTANT: These three aspects need to be constantly balanced and the boundaries between them understood and maintained. So many of the "don'ts" of pastoral care in this area involve respecting the difference between process, practical advice, and theological reflections, and not substituting a response from one area when what is called for is a response from another area. Religious advice without practical information can revictimize by dematerializing the problem of violence and ignoring its life-threatening nature. Practical information that neglects the spiritual crisis of trauma slights an important aspect of reconnecting with the source of the survivor's meaning and purpose. Inappropriate reactions will reinforce the idea that the minister cannot hear the experience that is causing them pain.

PROCESS

Ministers in their role as care providers appear to be saying to congregational members, "I am able to hear what you have to say." In offering some words about battering and abuse in a church context, ministers announce to victims that they have a specific concern about justice in this area. They are assuring victims or perpetrators who may approach them for help that they are aware of this problem and have some skill in dealing with it. They imply that they are able to monitor their own reactions and thus to help them. This is what I mean by *process*.

Empathy is essential. If ministers can recall an experience when they were afraid for their life, embarrassed to admit it, hesitant to seek help, then, appropriately they can feel empathy for the woman. But if ministers have never experienced such a life-threatening incident, then this empathy may be difficult to summon. Without this empathy, however, her words may become misinterpreted. Referring to a battered women's service as soon as possible will guarantee that this empathetic listening will occur.

Listening to what is being revealed can sometimes be disconcerting. Because the minister often knows both the perpetrator and the victim, what the woman reports about this familiar man and church member may seem unbelievable. Ministers may see him as a church elder, loving Sunday school teacher, and community business leader. They may not want to disturb this view of him. Ministers may need to believe things are not really so bad; such an observation, however, is meeting his or her own need, not the victim's.

Ministers may also need to believe that violence cannot happen to someone like themselves, that victims are unlike rather than similar to them. Thus ministers may hold the idea that victims come from poor families, or from families of a different race or ethnic group. They may need to protect some unrealistic image of their own race or ethnic group while holding to stereotypes about other racial or ethnic groups.

This need to believe that victims are unlike the ministers themselves may be achieved by focusing on the victim's—rather than the batterer's—behavior. Ministers need to be prepared to believe the unbelievable about him. Disbelief should not be conveyed, no matter how startling the information. Neither should the minister convey anger, because this could make the victim shift into the role of protecting her partner from the minister's anger.

If, when revealing details of her abuse, the victim realizes that her minister appears shocked or horrified, the message to her is that she has done something wrong, embarrassing, or incomprehensible. She has made the pastor uncomfortable. The care provider's inability to process this information in a less conspicuous manner creates a gulf between counselor and counselee. Becoming better informed about the behavior of abusive men makes the first encounter with someone who discloses her experience of abuse much less unnerving. Just as shock and horror are inappropriate in responding to a woman victim of battering, conveying anger, horror, fear, helplessness, or other responses that stigmatize is also inappropriate if a man who batters seeks help. Instead, concern needs to be conveyed even though the minister may feel the angry urge to confront, or even, to hurt the batterer.

PROVIDING PRACTICAL ASSISTANCE

Practical assistance is providing help to stop the battering behavior. Acquiring this practical information for responding to battered women and violent men requires a twofold approach with referral as its goal: first, being aware of the secular services available in the community; and second, feeling comfortable with referrals to these secular resources. To be comfortable with the role of referring, ministers need to see referral as caring, appropriate, and lifesaving.

Ministers may feel hesitant to refer the battering man or the battered woman to secular resources. Distrust of these resources is long-standing. Secular resources can appear to deny the validity and centrality of religious beliefs. But through cooperation, the church and secular services can enable one another to do what each does best, allowing the church to respond to the multitude of religious issues that battering raises.

Networking with colleagues in agencies to build trust and share resources helps to overcome the initial hesitancy attached to making referrals. Through this networking, ministers will learn of ongoing efforts to promote shelter's awareness and sensitivity to religious issues. Referrals need to be seen not as any admission of inadequacy, which they are not, but as an affirmation of the network of community resources that together can help keep women safe and hold men accountable for their behavior.

In responding to woman-battering, ministers need to be able to offer embodied and specific choices, saying to her,

> These are the choices you can make: You can seek legal help; you can obtain an order of protection; you can go to a shelter for battered women; you can join a battered women's support group;

and saying to him,

> You can enroll in a batterer's counseling program; you can cooperate with the prosecutor in seeing this case through the judicial system; you can develop alternatives to battering; you can begin to see how your behavior affects others; you can attempt to make restitution for what you have done; you can stop looking to her for caring; you can leave her alone.

The more qualitative and quantitative these practical choices are, the more helpful they will be. Undefined choices revictimize; informed choices empower.

THEOLOGICAL REFLECTIONS

Because of their theological training, ministers may short-circuit the search for practical information by providing only religious advice. Be aware that religious responses have long been used to justify battering and to avoid responding to battering. The minister is responsible for offering an alternative to these responses.

Lacking practical knowledge about ending abuse, ministers may feel that they can offer only religious advice. Thus, numerous battered women have complained that their pastors advised them to pray harder, to submit to their husbands, to be better Christian wives, to lift up the abuse to the Lord, to try to get their husbands to church. Without intervention that stops the abuse, these recommendations announce that the pastor is unable to help.

A situation that entraps a victim every day, affecting her material existence, is dematerialized when a religious response alone is offered. For instance, when clergy advise a woman to forgive the man who batters her, a religious response is substituted for a practical response. Forgiveness in the absence of repentance by the abuser is a salve for the conscience of the care provider but neither a healing experience nor safe for the victim.

The recommendation to forgive may result from the care provider's need for the woman to resolve or get over the abuse. Thus the minister's process needs are translated, inappropriately, into her religious needs. The option of forgiveness cannot be a medium for relieving care providers of a responsibility to address safety issues. It cannot mean, "You [the battered woman] forgive so that I [the minister] can forget about it." It is not a medium for discharging a time-consuming concern: hurry up and forgive (see Fortune 1991, 173–78), but it does reveal the way that process issues, practical issues, and religious concerns can become confused and result in ineffective or damaging responses. The goal is to offer an opportunity for theological reflections (see chapter 6).

At times, ministers may be approached by someone from a different church, confused because the only advice from her pastor there was advice about not breaking the covenant of marriage and an exhortation to stay with the man who is battering her. This advice offers only a religious response to a practical emergency and usually focuses on her need to improve her Christian characteristics (i.e., become more loving, more forgiving, more Christian, more prayerful), not on his need to stop his unchristian behavior. Often none of her safety needs has been addressed. In situations such as this, it is imperative to respond, with the issue of safety paramount, saying,

If you're being given advice to stay or submit because that is your duty, or because God ordains it, if you are told to forgive your husband without any sign that he has repented of his behavior, I would suggest an alternative. If you have been given this advice, no matter who the counselor is, no matter how inspiring or spiritually attuned he or she is, you have the wrong advisor for your specific needs at this time. It is not you who are mistaken for resisting this advice, it is the counselor who is mistaken for suggesting it. You have the right to be safe and God wants you to be safe.

ISSUES FOR MINISTRY

Clergy must be aware of specific issues that are raised in ministerial relationships and monitor their responses accordingly.

Gender Issues

If the minister is a man, the power dynamics of male-female roles are not escaped within counseling situations with battered women. Cultural forces influence any counseling relationship with women. "Cultural pressures on women to 'please men' are so profound that the woman's desire to be attractive and admired by her [minister] may override a more honest process of self-definition and self-determination" (Lerner 1988, 118). This is because, as Jean Baker Miller points out, members of subordinate groups become keenly aware of the expectations and interests of the dominant group (1976, 10–11).

In a counseling situation, the female victim—ever vigilant of silent clues and male behavior—may be alert to the male minister's expectations, substituting them for her own needs. A victim may consciously or unconsciously decide to please the male minister and assure him that she is nonthreatening. Indeed, this dependent, nonthreatening behavior may be rewarded by the counselor. Because of these gender issues as they impact counseling interactions, referral to a specialized battered women's service is essential. Male ministers can say, I don't want you to turn to another man who tells you what to do.

Moreover, like the batterer, male clergy may overidentify with the stereotypic male role and thus fail to challenge the controlling behavior of the batterer because it is seen as appropriate within an authoritarian model of the family. Most care providers were raised in a patriarchal hierarchical family, one in which the father's authority was secure and unchallenged, and they may unwittingly be playing that out in their own families now. This may temper the advice they give, inclining them to a conservatism that protects families rather than individual members. Egalitarian peer relationships between a care provider and his or her spouse provides an alternative to the authoritarian structure that reinforces a batterer's control and need to establish authority.

Ministers Who also Are Survivors

Some ministers may need to establish distance from the trauma story because of their own experience of victimization. If they were abused as a child, raped as an adolescent, or battered by a trusted partner, then this experience must be addressed before counseling others. Otherwise, ministers may project their own needs and responses onto those of the care seeker. They may numb themselves to stories of abuse and have difficulty in empathizing. They may not be able to maintain the self-monitoring process needed. They may not want to work in any capacity with the perpetrator. Ministers who are also survivors may fear the man who batters and be concerned for their own safety; a batterer may sense his power over the minister. These responses suggest the importance of making referrals.

If ministers have not consciously confronted and worked through the trauma of their own experience of abuse they may overidentify with the victim. Ministers may feel a need to rescue the care seeker and make decisions for her. They may project their needs and the resolution they desire on the care seeker's situation. They may feel helpless, reminded of their own victimization and unable to offer suggestions to protect the care seeker. They may minimize the seriousness of the abuse because this is the way they have handled their own suffering. Or they may verbally attack the victim and blame her for her situation because they have blamed themselves for their own victimization. In any of these instances, they become a wounded wounder (a term I first heard from Linda Hollies) rather than a wounded healer.

Ministers Who Have also Been Abusers

Ministers may have used violence to control their intimate partners and thus overidentify with the abuser. If ministers have not been consciously confronted and made accountable for this abusive behavior, and if they have not repented of this behavior and offered restitution, then they may be sympathetic to the claims of the abuser that the victim brought the violence upon herself. They may verbally attack the victim and blame her for her situation because they have placed the blame for their own abusive behavior on their partners. They may minimize the life-threatening nature of someone else's violence because they have minimized the life-threatening nature of their own violence.

Sexually Exploiting Her Vulnerability

As with survivors of child sexual abuse, battered women develop a finely tuned "sensitivity to the aggressor" (Kaschak 1992, 126). Like child sexual abuse survivors, battered women's longings for nurture and care may make it difficult to establish safe and appropriate boundaries with others. Their sensitive attunement to the controlling behavior of another makes them vulnerable to anyone in a position of power or authority. For this reason they are extremely susceptible to male clergy boundary violations.

Ministers may be attracted to the victim's vulnerability and thus be tempted to violate the professional boundary. Sadly, often when a woman comes to a care provider and reveals that she is being abused, the counselor initiates inappropriate sexual advances. Because of the extreme vulnerability of women being victimized and because of the continual violation of her boundaries by her partner, her neediness may be experienced by ministers in a sexualized way. She may be attracted to her care provider if she sees that person as gentle, caring, nonviolent, that is, an alternative to her partner.

IMPORTANT: The minister needs to recognize the great potential damage to the woman, should sexual boundaries be crossed by the minister. Violating boundaries by sexualizing the relationship not only corrupts the relationship but also confirms the abuser's demeaning reality to the victim, conveying, "There is no grace and no hope for grace; there is no one you can trust, not even your minister." This response offers exploitation instead of mutuality. It also endangers her.

Ministers need to recognize that men who batter are characterized by extraordinary possessiveness and delusional jealousy. Even if a care provider did not place the woman in a compromising position, the perpetrator might accuse her of having a relationship with her minister if he learns that she has sought counseling. Suspicions of lesbianism might be confirmed in his mind if she is seeing a woman minister. If ministers do violate professional boundaries, then they also confirm his distorted beliefs and provide another excuse for him to focus on her rather than on himself. Again, referral is called for.

Identification with the Batterer

The minister may be tempted to value the batterer's pain more highly than the victim's. It may feel easier to discount and discredit her pain. Her pain may be translated into being a bother or nuisance. Indeed, because of the erosion of her self by the man who batters, he may be more likable than she is. His pain may feel more immediate. Distinguishing between a good man in pain and someone who is required to face the consequences of his own actions can be difficult. Self-monitoring of one's sympathetic response to the batterer is essential.

The Discomfort of Calling to Accountability

Ministers may be discomforted by the idea of making the man experience the negative consequences of his battering behavior: helping him hear precise words about his violent actions and going through the criminal justice system. It may feel scary to say, "You are responsible for your behavior and I will not protect you from the consequences of that behavior." Ministers may confuse what caring means, thinking that taking care of people means making them feel better, when actually taking care of people is holding them responsible for their behavior (see Fortune and Poling 1993, 491).

Ministers must challenge the batterer's belief in his right to control a woman, his exercise of power, and his presumption of male privilege. This confrontational style can feel uncomfortable, but ministering to a man who batters means confronting him. Confronting him is a loving thing to do: first respectfully challenging his behavior and then ensuring that meaningful consequences are imposed.

An Active Counseling Role

David Switzer describes the active participation required of ministers in responding to crises: "questioning, searching, focusing, keeping the person on the present situation, interpreting, giving information, suggesting, mobilizing resources, and in calling for decision making." But, he cautions, "this is not as easy for many ministers as it may seem." The reason, he explains, is that "many of us tend to be rather passive in many situations and relationships, although not necessarily in all" (1986, 54–55). Upon hearing from either the victim or the perpetrator about life-threatening violence, the minister may think of all the appropriate responses, but due to this passivity, not be able to enact the appropriate responses.

Some ministers are fundamentally passive people. They feel uncomfortable saying, "What do you mean by that?" or, "I'm sorry, but I need to keep us on track." They feel more comfortable with being noninterruptive and nondirective. But this does not work with battering. Instead it allows a dangerous situation to prevail. Ministers must be ever alert to the perils of passivity.

Responding to battering requires initiative and assertiveness. For instance, if the victim is hospitalized by his battering behavior, go to her there. If the batterer is jailed for his behavior, then confronting him at the jailhouse and telling him that his incarceration offers an opportunity for him to repent of his battering behavior may be in order.

Feelings of Impatience

Ministers may be disheartened by the length of time it takes a battered woman to act according to what they think she should do (if indeed she does act this way). They may feel a strong desire that the problem be taken care of. Moreover, her help seeking may be experienced as inconvenient, her need for pastoral intervention felt to be ill-timed. Beware of unrealistic expectations and impatient responses.

Discomfort with the Criminal Justice System

Ministers may feel hesitant to use the criminal justice system. This hesitancy may be different for whites and people of color. White, middle-class people want to avoid the criminal justice system because they do not see it as relating to them; it challenges their self-image; and thus ministers who are white and middle class want to keep their people out of this system. People of color want to stay out of this system because they already know how the system treats them. Nevertheless, the use of the criminal justice system is in the woman's interest. This being so, it is also in the community's interest.

When a Woman Kills Her Abuser

Women who kill their abusers in self-defense represent a major theological hurdle for many church people. They ask, "How do we support the woman as she goes through the accounting of the criminal justice system without condoning the taking of life?"

In a sermon that addresses this issue, Marie Fortune advises, "Whenever any one of us takes the life of another human being, we should be called to account for our actions. It is the accounting we give that matters. Self-defense is the accounting to be given in this case" (1992, 130). In the face of physical threat or terror, individuals have the moral and legal right to defend themselves.

When a battered woman kills her husband in self-defense, this action announces the failure of the community to protect her. Indeed, Browne and Williams found that the availability of legal and extralegal resources (such as shelters and hotlines) is associated with a decline in the rate of female-perpetrated partner homicide (1989). But these resources must be accessible, responsive, and effective, and victims of battering must have both an awareness of them and the ability to mobilize them. Given this, the role of the church and its ministers in mediating resource availability and its use becomes even more urgent.

PASTORAL SELF-CARE

Ministers need an appropriate forum for exploring their reactions to woman-battering. Professional readiness involves recognizing that experiences of ministry will require debriefing and ensuring that a support network is in place at which this can occur.

Ministers will need such a support network for many reasons:

- Confronting the reality of evil in stories of cruelty can undermine one's faith.
- Hearing of battering behavior may heighten one's own sense of vulnerability.

- One may become isolated, thinking that the situation can be handled individually, thus mimicking the isolation of both the perpetrator and the victim.
- One may feel helpless, and overcompensate for this feeling by becoming her rescuer, thus sending her the wrong message. Instead of having her capabilities affirmed and receiving appropriate referrals, her helplessness is emphasized. Thus she is patronized rather than empowered.
- One may find oneself becoming skeptical of her story, judgmental of her behavior if it is not what was desired that she do, feeling contempt for her failure to act, identifying with his pain rather than hers. The church and community's view of the two of them may become too influential.
- One may be fantasizing about violating the boundaries of the pastoral relationship.
- One may become emotionally and physically drained by encounters with woman-battering, and although the church often sends a message that taking care of oneself is not a priority, it is. Beware of emotional fatigue—it helps no one. Self-nurture is essential; support groups are sources of encouragement for self-nurture.
- Understanding the possible reactions and being in touch with feelings such as grief, rage, bitterness, depression, anger, frustration is often easier in the midst of a supportive group.
- It may be difficult to accept ambiguity when what is desired is clear-cut responses.
- One may feel anxious by the image of God that a woman abused by her husband holds (a hypervigilant, punishing God) and want to banish that image rather than creating the space for a woman's experience of God to be expressed.

For all these reasons a safe place for debriefing, exploring, and being supported is essential.

As ministers acquire practical information about community resources, they may discover people who could form a part of their support network and to whom they can turn for assistance, educational information, help in processing emotional responses to woman-battering, or assistance in maintaining professional boundaries and exploring gender issues in counseling.

Besides ensuring the existence of a supportive group presence, ministers should not neglect taking their reactions and feelings to God through prayer. Meditation and prayer during times of counseling victims or abusers will be an important aspect of the counseling and spiritual life. Learning about the horrors of abusive behavior will force ministers to expand their understanding of what is humanly possible in terms of evil. This will affect them both theologically and emotionally; prayer will be one among many valuable ways to respond to the evil to which they are now exposed.

3

MAKING REFERRALS

Men who batter often isolate themselves and their victims. This isolation deprives both of personal support systems, and keeps victims from identifying or finding sources of protection. The social network a woman may have at the beginning of a relationship is steadily eroded, resulting in increasing isolation. The decreasing social network not only works to isolate the victim, but to increase her susceptibility to accepting the abuser's interpretations of the reasons he is abusive (it is her fault, he could not help it, he has been empowered by God) and his representations of the larger community as supporting him or not caring about her. The woman's help-seeking efforts must be understood within the context represented by the spiral of her abuser's controlling efforts. That is, she is increasingly isolated and her social networks eroded during a time when she most needs such support.

The minister may be the couple's link from this isolation to support, from his complete dependency on the relationship to a healthy acceptance of a friendship and family network. The minister's role in this transition from isolation is not as the final destination but as the terminal that connects them to the necessary resources, thus expanding their associations and providing alternatives to isolation.

ARGUMENTS AGAINST COUPLE COUNSELING

When a woman reveals that she is being battered, the seemingly helpful response may seem obvious: Get the two of them together, and help them work out the problem. This obvious response to battering, especially if it involves congregational members, while understandable, is erroneous. It does correspond with the orientation of traditional pastoral counseling, working with the family or the couple. But a difference exists between marital conflict and abusive relationships. By responding with an offer of couple counseling, the minister assumes the role of final destination rather than connection terminal. The offer also reinforces the idea that private resolutions to violence are effective when they are not.

When a man is violent against his partner, the abuse is his responsibility and his alone. The abused person can do little or nothing to stop the violence. To address the issue of violence within the context of some form of couple counseling disperses the culpability, minimizing the life-threatening nature of the violence and allowing it to dissolve into relationship issues. Couple counseling incorrectly assumes that the battered woman's presence is necessary in order to help the man who batters to cease using violence.

Couple counseling presumes an equal relationship, in which neither person is afraid to voice his or her own perspective. In fact, in a relationship with a man who batters, one person holds power over the other. Because of this power inequity, there is no reason for them to tell the minister the truth. In fact, each person has reasons to lie: she because she fears for her safety, and he because denial and minimization are a part of the mechanism of abusive behavior.

One clergyperson who specialized in family therapy described a situation in which months of couple counseling had gone by with no progress. He was confused by this. Then, the couple stopped coming for sessions. Only later, after they divorced, did the wife confide to him that her husband had been battering her for years. At the last session she had sat throughout the session bleeding into her hair from a head wound. Just before they left to see the minister, her husband had rammed her head against a wall with a nail protruding from it. None of his abusive behavior was ever addressed in couple's counseling, because the clergyperson did not know to look for it, and neither of them initiated a discussion of it.

Couple Counseling Threatens the Batterer

Remember that battering establishes control, and loss of control is precisely what a batterer fears. Because a third person is present, the abuser is threatened with loss of control. Although the victim may be ostensibly safe from the abuser's violence during the hour or so that they are together in a pastor's study, this counseling experience itself may heighten tensions. If a man batters his wife when he is anxious, and the content of the marriage counseling increases his anxiety, then counseling can increase the likelihood of violence rather than decreasing it. A man may batter his partner just prior to or immediately after a counseling session. As Anne Ganley reports, "In my practice, a significant portion of the couples who had received traditional marital counseling reported that the sessions were often followed by battering episodes" (Ganley 1981, 39).

Couple Counseling Endangers the Battered Woman

The dynamics that create the legitimacy for the perpetrator to commit violence do not end within the walls of the minister's office. In fact, bringing the two together works to reinforce control—the abuser continues to be present, monitoring all that she says and does. Either the woman becomes compliant to her abuser in counseling and says nothing about the violence or tells the truth and faces the consequences afterward. Remember, what she reveals in public, she will pay for later in private. Even if ministers recognize an imbalance of power, they cannot equalize this imbalance simply by their presence. The woman will always be in danger for what she reveals, and the abuser will always encourage collusion between himself and the clergyperson.

Other Reasons for Refusing Couple Counseling

The battered woman may request couple counseling because she wants the abuse to stop, and agreeing to joint counseling may seem to be the only way to get him to seek help. Batterers will always try to get their partners to attend counseling with them, often making their own participation conditional on their partner's participation. Many women agree to this—happy that their partners will consider any therapy.

Skilled in manipulation, a perpetrator may choose to participate in couple counseling because he believes that the clergyperson can be won over to his perspective. Not only does he continue his pattern of denial by displacing his responsibility for the violence onto her but he also will manipulate the situation so that the minister will be more likely to identify with his pain rather than hers. Motivated by desperation that the situation may change and his access to the victim be denied, he may present to the clergyperson a demeanor both harmless and caring.

Exquisitely in control, he will appeal to a minister's desire to mediate. He does this by denying her perspective, one aspect of emotional abuse. He argues that she is too sensitive, that she exaggerates his behavior, that she is imagining things, that she is the one who is ill, that she is hysterical. This can appear to a counselor as a difference of opinion, who then assumes the role of mediation. Not only is this behavior abusive, but it actively denies the role of the abuser—she may, indeed, be hysterical after he has hit her (see Jones and Schecter 1992). Mediation when abusive behavior exists in a relationship is inappropriate.

Couple counseling does not help advance an important goal for this relationship: Both individuals need to be able to separate their identities from each other. Rather than be seen and treated as a couple, they need to be seen and treated as two individuals. Counseling apart from each other—by specialized service providers for battered women and battering men—is required to help them begin to see themselves as capable of acting independently.

If the woman has left the batterer, then he may propose couple counseling because he sees it as an avenue for getting her back. Many clinical studies confirm that most batterers were motivated to attend counseling to get their wives back. As soon as the threat of separation is over they drop out, feeling more powerful by their success at her return (see Gondolf and Fisher 1988, 87).

Finally, abusers need to be constantly confronted, in a group setting, by other abusers and an experienced therapist. This situation alone reduces the ability of the abuser to collude with an individual counselor in order to minimize his own responsibility for his violence. If the abuser is called on his be-havior by the minister, then he may simply stop coming to the counseling sessions under the pretense of increased work demands or an injury or charg-ing that the minister is inadequate.

A REFERRAL MODEL FOR PASTORAL CARE

Before a woman approaches a minister for assistance, she has probably tried for some time to fix the situation herself; generally she does this by accom-modating behavior. The coping skills a woman develops in the face of a bat-tering attack, such as minimizing the potential lethality (It was only a push, a slap, a broken nose), denying the agency (He didn't mean to do it), and ac-cepting accountability (I should have done . . .), leave the actions unchal-lenged and the man who batters unaccountable. In other words, she has adopted an interpersonal response to the battering. Couple counseling reca-pitulates at the pastoral care level the same interpersonal response that she had attempted on her own. What is needed instead is referral to appropriate community resources.

Just as the battering behavior is something that the victim herself cannot stop, requiring instead outside sanctions and accountability, so the couple's conflicting needs require a response greater than the church's, namely, com-munity sanctions for him, safety for her. The church cannot stop battering on its own, solely through its representatives. Instead, the intervention of the larger community is essential. Battering, after all, is a crime. The minister's role is to help victims and perpetrators to understand the importance of a co-ordinated community response as the only way truly to protect and call to accountability.

Clergy are in a unique position as counselors because they carry a symbolic power. As David Switzer explains, "quite apart from their own being as per-sons, clergy are perceived by others as being the physical representation to the community of faith and, at least to some extent, to the larger community of the reality of God" (1986, 16). Because ministers are a symbol of something else—the church, God, Christ—they may assume that the weight of the pas-toral office will be sufficient in and of itself to stop the abuser. But this as-sumption is incorrect. The symbolic value of the minister's office may be a help and should be used to communicate that his controlling, abusive behav-ior must stop—but it is insufficient alone. The abuser needs to hear the same message, that the abuse is wrong and must stop, from as many authorities as possible. When he hears this message from his partner "*and* the marriage counselor *and* the minister *and* some friends *and* the police *and* the judge *and* his father *and* his boss all at once, then he may get the message that his controlling behavior isn't going to work any more" (Jones and Schecter 1992, 96).

The more people who tell the abuser that his behavior is not going to work any more, who make him take responsibility for his abusive behavior, and the more serious the consequences of his actions (an order of protection, court-ordered counseling, being left by his partner, being sentenced to jail, being fired from his job), the more he is likely to see that his abuse is not working. These external forces offer an opportunity for internal change and a reason for change. See Figure 2, Community Accountability Wheel.

A referral model for pastoral care acknowledges that the community—not the church, not the clergyperson, not the couple, not the woman—is the locus for bringing about change. The community has been empowered to provide sanctions for battering behavior through the criminal justice system.

How the Community Responds to the Batterer's Needs

The abusive man needs aversive consequences that tell him battering behavior will no longer work and that hold him legally accountable for this behavior. The community provides these through arrest, sentencing, and serving jail time, or being ordered to attend a batterer's group.

The man who batters may prefer to have the minister deal with his problem. He may gravitate to the language of Christian repentance or conversion as a means of regaining or maintaining control over the victim and deceiving the minister. Because he is sophisticated at manipulation, he is found believable by the victim and their minister. Thus, keeping the problem of battering within the church context usually plays into the perpetrator's manipulative behavior.

The community has more resources to respond to the perpetrator's needs than does the church. Groups for batterers are extremely valuable in addressing the issues of violence and control. If they are doing a good job, these groups confront and address the issues of power and control. Groups for men who batter help develop alternatives to battering behavior: time-outs, empathizing, problem-solving, tension-reducing exercises, addressing issues of anger, increasing their understanding of the family and the social facilitators of woman-battering, increasing identification and expression of all feelings. Such groups also decrease isolation and decrease dependency on the relationship by helping to develop a personal support system. Nevertheless, just changing the behavior will not stop the battering. Groups must also confront the batterer's assumptions about his partner. Batterers' groups should be led by therapists who have experience in treating abusers, naming violence, and working toward ending emotional, physical, and sexual violence. The batterer must be challenged first to change, and after changing, to make restitution. He must stop looking to her for caring and begin to ask himself always, Is what I want fair?

When a man batters (and, in most states, when he rapes) his wife, he has violated the law. The sooner the criminal justice system is brought into the

Figure 2: Community Accountabilty Wheel

MEDIA WILL: educate the community about the epidemic of violence against women; prioritize safety, equal opportunity, and justice for women and children over profit, popularity, and advantage; expose and condemn patriarchal privilege, abuse, secrecy, and chauvinism; cease its practice of glorifying violence against women and children.

SOCIAL SERVICE PROVIDERS WILL: become social change advocates for battered women; refer batterers to accountable intervention programs; stop blaming batterers' behavior on myths such as drugs and alcohol, family history, anger, provocation, "loss of control"; design and deliver services which are sensitive to women and children's safety needs; minimize how batterers use them to continue their battering of their families.

LEGISLATORS WILL: pass laws which define battering by men as criminal behavior *without exception;* pass laws which vigorously and progressively sanction men's battering behavior; pass laws which create standards for accountable batterer intervention programs; pass laws requiring coordinated systems of intervention in domestic violence; provide ample funding to accomplish its goal of eradicating domestic violence.

EMPLOYERS WILL: condition batterer's continuing employment on remaining nonviolent; actively intervene against men's stalking in the workplace; support, financially and otherwise, advocacy and services for battered women and children; continually educate and dialogue, through personnel services, about domestic violence issues.

JUSTICE SYSTEM WILL: adopt mandatory arrest policy for men who batter; charge and prosecute batterers in a manner that does not rely on the victims' involvement; refer batterers exclusively to intervention programs which meet state or federal standards; never offer delayed or deferred sentence options to batterers; provide easily accessible protection orders and back them up; incarcerate batterers for noncompliance of any aspect with their adjudication.

EDUCATORS WILL: dialogue with students about violence in their homes the dynamics of domestic violence, and how it is founded on the oppression of women and the worship of men; provide a leadership role in research and theoretical development which prioritizes gender justice, equal opportunity, and peace; intervene in harassment, abuse, violence, and intimidation of girls/women in the education system.

CLERGY WILL: conduct outreach into the congregation regarding domestic violence and provide a safe environment for women to discuss their experiences; develop internal policies for responding to domestic violence; speak out against domestic violence from the pulpit; organize multi-faith coalitions to educate the religious community; actively interact with the existing domestic violence intervention community.

MEN WILL: acknowledge that all men benefit from men's violence; oppose men's violence; use peer pressure to stop violence against women and children; make peace, justice, and equality masculine virtues; vigorously confront men who indulge in misogynistic behavior; seek out and accept the leadership of women.

The Community Accountability Wheel has been adapted from a wheel developed for the Domestic Violence Institute of Michigan, P.O. Box 130107, Ann Arbor, MI 48113-0107. Used by permission. On the original wheel, the text appears within the spaces between the spokes.

process of creating accountability the better. Learn local arrest policies. The legal instrument that instructs the abuser to stay away from and stop harming his victim is often called an *order of protection* (it might be called an *injunction* or *restraining order*). Ministers should learn what this instrument is called in their state and the steps a woman must take to obtain one. Also, in some states, orders of protection only apply if a woman has separated from her abuser. Do state orders of protection become invalid if the woman reconciles with her husband? Who can get orders of protection and whom do these orders of protection protect?

How Battered Women's Services Respond

A woman harmed by her partner has been made extremely vulnerable. She can no longer assume that she is safe within the walls of her own house; she must be ever vigilant; she cannot trust her partner; she must strategize with her children for their joint safety. Battered women's services will assist her in this and address her needs to develop the capacity to protect herself.

The victim needs to *be safe*. Battered women's services attempt to guarantee safety (only infrequently do batterers discover their location); the church cannot guarantee such safety. Shelters are also expert at responding to the pleadings of batterers and know how to work with the criminal justice system. She also needs to make plans for how to *stay* safe. Battered women's services can provide assistance in planning for safety.

Battered women's shelters are consistently rated by battered women as the most helpful resource. Studies have shown that *"using a women's shelter reduces a woman's risk of being beaten again, whether or not she returns to her partner"* (Luepnitz 1988, 67). Most shelters provide twenty-four-hour-a-day shelter and crisis hotline, legal assistance, referral to community services, counseling, support, confidential support groups, legal advocacy, referral to medical care, emergency transportation, and services for children (including baby-sitting, children's counseling, and attention to children's education needs). Shelters take the pressure off families or friends whom the abuser might approach, and, unlike families and friends, have experience keeping women and children safe. Shelters offer a place where encounters with other women with similar experiences can occur. Comfort, community, and strategic feedback are available here. The women there understand why a woman sometimes chooses to go back, and let her know that she can come back when she needs to. The staff of shelters are valuable resources in themselves and know of the additional resources in the community.

Women may choose not to enter a shelter for many reasons (It's not in my children's school district, I would be ashamed, I don't see myself like those "other women," It's not my home, I have other family resources or other financial resources), but they may use the other shelter program resources to establish a safety plan, break their isolation, network, and take legal actions, such as obtaining an order for protection.

The battered woman needs to talk with others who have suffered violence from their partners. The need for a support network is necessary given the erosion of her social network by the batterer's controlling behavior. Support groups for battered women help to overcome the isolation imposed by the batterer, affirming to the individual—"You are not alone. You can do it"— because others have struggled with the problem too. They permit the telling of shameful secrets within a reciprocal process that allows each woman to reach out to others and to receive from others. They foster strength, bear witness, and allow for the expression of grief. In a group situation they can realize that their suffering does not invalidate their ability to give and receive. Their peers can point out the fantasy of certain expectations (He is going to change. Things are going to get better) because they have had them too (I thought that too, but it wasn't true because he had no reason to change—I came back too soon!).

HOW TO REFER

Most clergy do not have specialized skills in the area of woman-battering, but as generalist counselors they have sufficient skills to guide the care seeker to the appropriate resources. Referral to a battered women's service relieves clergy of having to learn and retain all the vital information about safety concerns that she needs to consider; yet it ensures that relevant safety issues get covered. Referral affirms to the battered woman, the battering man, and to the minister that battering is a community concern, that there are many allies in working to stop violence. It also allows ministers to do what they do best: address the religious crisis of battering.

Consider an evangelism model for the community-wide response that is required in responding to the man who batters: The church does not see itself as offering only one opportunity for its evangelism to work. Instead, it offers Sunday school and Bible study, perhaps community outreach programs, pastoral visits, and of course worship services. Through all of these different activities, the message is conveyed that God cares about individuals and that the church is a place where people of God come together. Similarly, through the united efforts of the justice system, the battered women's program, a network of family and friends, as well as the church, the message is communicated: We care about you, and your abusive behavior must stop. This evangelism of anti-battering, this community-wide leveraging of help, is absolutely essential.

Know the Local Resources

At the end of this book is a tool to assist ministers in assessing their community's resources: the Local Resources list on page 127. In filling it out, ministers will gain a sense of secular resources that can be called upon for referral and networking. Clip or copy the Local Resources list and have it in an accessible place. It ensures that ministers know the local resources, such as food pantries, housing, emergency housing, financial assistance, and so forth. Be sure to learn how to make referrals. For instance, how does Aid to Families with Dependent Children (AFDC) work? Who is eligible for public housing? Develop a resource list of local programs, shelters, hotlines, free legal aid, self-defense classes, and assertiveness classes to give to battered women. Develop a separate resource list for batterers that omits any information regarding specific services for battered women. IMPORTANT: Check all referrals before using them or putting them on the resource list for congregational members.

Working with Battered Women's Services

Prior to naming battering in a congregational setting, arrange to meet someone from the nearest battered women's shelter or specialized service, even if it is quite a distance away. Because many battered women's shelters keep their location private, and because shelters may prefer that a male minister not visit the shelter itself, call and ask to speak to one of their outreach workers or counselors. Ministers need to explain that they realize that there are battered women in their congregation and they wish to be prepared to help them. Request an appointment with someone from the battered women's service to learn what their services are, and how best to work with them to help battered women in the congregation. Ask how referrals are made. In most cases, the service providers will be delighted to hear from a minister who wants to work with them to provide safety for women and children. They will arrange a meeting at a location that protects the confidentiality of their clients.

Most women, unless in an emergency situation, first check out the shelter program by calling the hotline. Many women may use one or two of the services offered by a domestic violence program outside of the shelter itself; they may use a shelter advocate for help maneuvering through the legal system for protection orders, or the support group. Women will use different pieces of a shelter or domestic violence program in different ways, and at different times, and using program services does not always start with emergency shelter. Be familiar enough with the basic services of the local programs so that the referral is not framed as though it requires leaving home and moving into a shelter.

Affirming the Value of Prosecution

Prosecution is one of the most effective ways to curtail battering, especially when linked with court-ordered counseling for the batterer. It is appropriate to say to the woman, "Would you like me or someone you trust from the church to be with you when you meet with the police?" This establishes several things: that what has transpired is against the law (that is, the legal system has an interest in protecting women in the home); that prosecution for this offense is entirely legitimate and acceptable; and that the woman does not need to be isolated in going through the legal system.

Specialized Treatment Referrals

Refer the victims or abusers for any specialized treatment they need, but do not confuse their needs for specialized treatment with the problem of battering behavior. For instance, do not confuse the problem of alcohol or drug addiction that some victims or abusers have with the problem of battering behavior. Treatment of the abuser's alcohol or drug addiction, while an important and a necessary step in stopping the battering behavior, does not in itself reduce the threat of battering. Treatment of the victim's addiction, especially if it is developed as a coping mechanism to the battering, does nothing to guarantee her safety. Intervention must address the problem of addiction concurrently, but not in the place of intervention for battering behavior.

The woman may require counseling around reproductive issues. Referring her to a local Planned Parenthood or similar agency while also recommending that she should get a complete physical examination are ways of affirming that her body is a temple of God that should be cared for and healed.

Refer a potentially suicidal person to a suicide prevention resource. But, again, do not think that suicide intervention will end the chronic problem of battering.

Responding to Child Abuse

Because physical and sexual child abuse frequently occur in homes where a man batters his partner, ministers may become aware that the battering man or the battered woman has abused one or more of their children. The woman seeking help needs to be assured that her revelations shall be kept confidential, with one exception. Ministers need to make it clear that they will report any information about harm to a child to Child Protective Services (CPS). If ministers do learn from a battered woman about child abuse, they should feel comfortable using consultation with other professionals in the field to ensure that all options are identified and that safety issues remain the primary concern.

The goals for responding to the victims and the abusers in cases of child sexual abuse and child physical abuse are similar to the goals for responding to woman-battering:

1. Protect the safety of the child, while also ensuring the safety of the mother. The minister may live in a state where he or she is mandated to report instances of child abuse to the state's CPS. Ministers should

see themselves as ethically mandated to report, and be prepared to report (see Fortune 1991, 225–33 for a discussion). Call CPS and learn the protocol for reporting a case.

2. If ministers learn of harm to a child from either the battered woman or the man who hurts her, they should encourage her or him to report this harm to CPS in their presence. This self-reporting is one form of accepting responsibility for protecting the interests of the vulnerable child. The minister's presence during the phone call or meeting also confirms that support will continue throughout the process. Whether she is self-reporting or the minister makes the report, CPS should be informed that the mother is also a victim of abuse.

IMPORTANT: With the involvement of a state agency, the woman's safety and the children's safety are seriously compromised. The minister should ensure that the mother herself remains safe. If the woman is not self-reporting, then the minister needs to be sure that she is aware of the minister's plans to call CPS. *She must have a safety plan in place.* Given this, referral to a battered women's program becomes even more essential, so that she has trained professionals working with her to ensure the safety of herself and her children.

IMPORTANT: Besides calling the police if an emergency call is interrupted (see Appendix, Handling an Emergency Call, on p. 119), this is the only time that the confidentiality of the battered woman should be breached, and in each case she should be told that a call will be made.

3. Hold the abuser accountable for the violence and ensure that it is stopped.

4. Address the material and spiritual needs of the child separate from the needs of the family. Until the child is guaranteed to be safe, the minister's main concern must be to address each of the individuals in the family as individuals rather than the family itself as a unit.

PROACTIVE PASTORAL CARE

Ministers need to see themselves as part of a team of community responses, working with secular resources such as the criminal justice system and battered women's shelters. They can say to either the victim or the batterer: I appreciate that you shared this with me, but this is a problem we cannot solve ourselves.

In the place of a traditional model of pastoral care we need specifically a proactive model in response to violence. (See Table 3, Proactive Pastoral Care.)

The anchors for this referral model of proactive pastoral care are affirmations that speak to the validity of each person's help-seeking. Affirmations are

Table 3: Proactive Pastoral Care	
Traditional Model	*Proactive Model*
"Relationship" issues	Safety issues
Getting them to talk about their interpersonal problems	Accountability for battering behavior
Dematerializing the crisis by focusing solely on religious issues	Focus on both physical and spiritual trauma
"Lone Ranger" counseling	Referrals, including criminal justice system, shelter
	Affirming that change is possible
Personal problem	Community problem

valuable for both practical and spiritual purposes. Affirmations can be powerful ways of communicating faith in the victim's or the perpetrator's ability to change, and restoring faith in themselves. Ministers can affirm the value of receiving appropriate help. Affirmations that center on the idea that change is possible (You can change your life, You deserve a nonviolent life, You can respond in other ways than battering) should be coupled with practical information that allows each person to enact this change.

Affirmations normalize the victim's care seeking. Ministers can affirm that disclosing the violence to appropriate resources can help to protect her. They can tell her that secular resources exist in her community because God and her community do not want her to come to harm. To the woman, they can also say:

- Wanting change is a sign of strength.
- Seeking help is an act of courage.
- You have the right to a life free from violence.
- You are not responsible for the battering.
- You are not going to go hungry, and I shall ensure that this is true.

To the man who batters they can offer affirmations, such as:

- You can change your behavior.
- You are not out of control.
- You are not crazy.
- I care enough about you to tell you your battering behavior has to stop and only you can stop it.

These affirmations grow from the soil of practical advice, advice that provides specific information on the ways changes can occur, and who in the community can help make change possible. This is proactive pastoral care at its best.

Safety First

In addition to affirmations, some guidelines for responding to woman-battering need to be kept in mind. Once a minister learns of woman-battering, the primary goal that must be pursued is to ensure the victim's safety. Safety is the paramount concern because of the life-threatening nature of any one battering incident. Ministers must always consider the possibility of a fatal outcome. Their capacity to intervene involves "anticipating the worst and preparing for it" (Hilberman 1980, 1344). If they receive an emergency call regarding a battering incident, they should use the Appendix (Handling an Emergency Call on p. 119). Exploring safety issues is a specialized skill; battered women's programs can ensure that safety planning is in place.

Challenge the Battering Behavior

Do not focus on the qualities of either the victim or the abuser in determining whether battering occurred (e.g., "She asked for it." "But he's such a great person"). Not the characteristics, but the behaviors define battering (Ganley 1981). Whether working with the victim or the abuser, do not spend time determining whether or not battering is justified. It never is. Regardless of any problem the relationship may or may not have, other solutions should be used. Violence is not a solution to relationship problems. Not the motive or the cause of battering is the concern, but the behavior (Ganley 1981). Another way to think of this is: It is his verbs and adverbs (pushing, hit, slapped, raped); not her nouns and adjectives (nagging, unchristian), or his nouns and adjectives (veteran, alcoholic).

IMPORTANT: Unequivocally challenge the behavior. Be ready to use clerical authority immediately to hold the abuser accountable. Accountability includes stopping the abusive behavior and accepting the consequences of his behavior.

Because battering behavior is learned, it can be unlearned. For a perpetrator to successfully end his violence takes a long time. Several weeks of counseling is insufficient. Even some time in jail may be inadequate. The way in which he interprets his own behavior must be challenged or change will not occur.

4

SAFETY

A hospital chaplain called upon a woman who had just given birth. There had been no complications with the birth, and the chaplain began what he thought would be a routine discussion. He was shocked and distressed when the woman told him that she was afraid to return home, that her husband battered her, and that she was terrified of what would happen to her and her baby. Not knowing what to do, the chaplain gave her his home phone number (he lived in a community forty miles away) and encouraged her to call him if she needed help when she returned home.

Clearly, this person—although caring and wanting to help—was unable to be of any assistance. Indeed, such a response could have derailed her efforts to seek help by leaving the impression that this was all the assistance that she would need or that he could offer. Fortunately in this case the chaplain reported the woman's terror to another chaplain at the hospital. This second chaplain scheduled a meeting for her with the hospital's social worker, who then made arrangements for her to go to a shelter for battered women.

WHY BATTERED WOMEN SEEK PASTORAL CARE

While both the battered woman and the battering man feel pain and confusion, chances are that the minister will be contacted for help by the victim rather than the perpetrator. He fears that she will leave; she fears that he may kill her next time. She may also feel devastated, demeaned, humiliated, degraded, despondent, depressed, shocked, defiled, betrayed, isolated, entrapped, guilty, powerless. She may be worried about whether she can ever trust men again. For some women, turning to a clergyperson is often a logical step in response to these feelings. Moreover, after guiding families through such crises as illness, marriage, births, and deaths, ministers become trusted and known. They are often the first people approached in a crisis.

She may be motivated to seek help from ministers for several other reasons as well: The church may be the only social outlet allowed her. The man who batters may view the church with such contempt or apathy that he does not worry about her activities in the church. Or he may be an active member and encourage her church activity because he sees it as a place that confirms his claims about a husband's authority and a wife's obedience. Or the abuser may forbid her from going to church and this prompts her to seek help.

Battering and marital rape provoke spiritual crises that secular resources cannot address. Due to the chronic trauma she is experiencing from someone she loves, questions of faith inevitably arise. Her relationship with God has been profoundly altered. Seeking an answer to the question, Why me? raises issues of guilt, responsibility, and suffering. In the face of harm and the threat of harm, she may have constructed a theological explanation for her situation that focuses on her sinfulness, her need to suffer, and divine retributive punishment. She thus may be imprisoned within the control of a batterer and a theological construct in which God frighteningly resembles the batterer—a God who gives conditional love, punishes, has absolute standards, and is rigid and unforgiving. She may be seeking an understanding of this hyper-vigilant God or an understanding of an absent God who abandons her in her need and leaves her cries for help unanswered.

She may be confused about what her marriage vows require of her in the face of battering. She may feel responsible for the success or failure of the relationship. She may not know where else to turn or, conversely, she may be seeking help everywhere.

Ministers are available. They can see someone quickly; no one has to wait months for an appointment. Parish clergy usually do not charge for counseling, thus she will not have to file insurance claims that could notify the man who batters that help-seeking is taking place.

She assumes that ministers hear many secrets and thus protect confidentialities. She knows that if someone revealed confidentialities about her abusive partner that it might endanger her. Or, she may decide a minister can help them, and she talks her partner into getting counseling together.

IMPORTANT: Whatever reason brings her into contact with a minister, at that point, the minister becomes one of the variables in her quest for safety.

RESPONDING RESPONSIBLY

The first essential, absolute requirement for ministers is simple and straightforward: Do not tell anyone. Do not break the woman's confidence or discuss the situation with the woman's partner. Do not say to a batterer or anyone else, I referred her to a shelter, I think she went to her aunt's, and so forth.

IMPORTANT: Ministers must remember at all times that providing any information to someone else about her can endanger her life. Several other responses could further endanger her:

• Do not advise her or exhort her to stay in an abusive situation. This would put the woman, and her children if she has any, in danger.

- Do not case manage her life for her, taking over the decision-making.
- Do not make the assumption that this marriage should be kept together at all costs.
- Do not respond by displacing the focus from his responsibility for his behavior by saying, "Tell me about your family history," or "What did you do to provoke him?" reinforcing in these questions that it is somehow because of her that the violence is occurring.
- Do not trivialize or minimize what has occurred. Be concerned about any injuries she has, and be alert to her coping mechanism of minimizing body injuries. Women tune out their own physical ailments as a survival mechanism. Encourage her to get pictures of any injuries to be used in court.
- Be aware that one's own expectations for action may result in judging the battered woman's struggle for survival as inaction.
- Remember that leaving a batterer and/or achieving safety is a long process. Once a minister has outlined the perceived options and community resources, it does not mean that the battered woman will react immediately, or according to the minister's expectations.
- Refer as soon as possible, involving all appropriate secular resources (especially shelters and the police).

The primary emphasis in response to the disclosure of the battering is, first and foremost, to ensure the safety of the victim of the abuse. Other issues about the relationship, such as divorce, must be subordinated to the issue of violence. If the woman identifies the abuse as the first incident (meaning the first physical incident), then one should assume a prior history of emotional and psychological abuse (hands-off battering), which are also tactics used by the abuser to maintain power and control in the relationship. She is now experiencing physical or sexual abuse as an escalation in her batterer's tactics, which is part of his larger pattern of controlling behaviors. Using Figure 1 on p. 18, Power and Control Wheel, can help her put this hands-off battering into the context of his physical violence. The counseling should be characterized by these ingredients: caring, concern for safety, empowerment, and referral.

Caring

Ministers can say, "I am sorry this happened to you; how scary that must have been." She has been courageous in breaking the silence; this should be acknowledged. She should be told no one ever deserves to be hit or hurt. Ministers can affirm that her reactions are normal; she is not going crazy even though she has never experienced such a range of emotions before. Ministers can validate these feelings: It is all right to feel betrayed, hurt, angry, and so forth. Caring questions might include, "How are you doing?" and "Are you able to rest at night?" Ministers begin by listening to her, by caring, by valuing her opinions, and supporting her.

Concern for Safety

Immediately, however, ministers must acknowledge the trauma and life-threatening nature of battering. The violence must be unequivocally challenged. Women must be encouraged to take their husband's violence seriously and to find support for challenging this violence. Their duty is not to submit to their husband's physical or sexual violence.

Questions that focus on safety issues need to be asked, such as, What would it take for you to be safe? Hospital chaplains who learn that the injuries that resulted in hospitalization were inflicted by her male partner can say:

> I am sorry this has happened to you. It is not your fault. But we need to talk about what will happen when you are released from the hospital and how you can be safe.

It may be necessary to help her see the urgency of her situation. IMPORTANT: Trust the woman to know what is safe for her, and help her figure out her options, but do not impose expectations on her.

Empowerment

She should be reassured that it is possible to reestablish control over her life. She has choices. Resources are available. She could benefit from creating new support systems, expanding her problem-solving skills, and increasing her sense of responsibility toward herself. Ministers can help her understand her alternatives while increasing her sense of control. They can ask, "What decisions have you made so far? What are your concerns?"

Say to her, "I have some books on the subject that I would like you to know about." Then show her Ann Jones and Susan Schecter's *When Love Goes Wrong* and Ginny NiCarthy's *Getting Free*. Give her a copy to keep of Marie Fortune's *Keeping the Faith*. Because they speak directly to women in their situations—addressing questions from the practical to the theological—these books empower in several ways. They announce that she is not alone in seeking help; they validate the theological and emotional questions she may have by answering them. They provide a framework for recognizing the patterns of abuse and offer practical advice for responding to the chronic problem of battering. They also indicate that while the church is a resource, there are other resources as well.

It is important to acknowledge that the destruction of the marriage has already occurred; the husband's battering behavior has destroyed the covenantal nature of the marriage. Separation to achieve safety acknowledges that the covenant is broken, but it is not the act that breaks the covenant (see

Eilts 1988). Ministers should affirm, "These are your decisions to make. But I am concerned about your safety and I can see that you are as well." She should be encouraged to see her right to be free of violence as a theological imperative.

Because expanding her network of support is so essential, help her identify who can support her and how she can feel stronger. Ask her what she will do when she leaves the counseling session. "Don't be surprised if she feels safer taking no action. Do not mistake her strategy of doing nothing for passivity or indifference" (Jones and Schecter 1992, 310). The minister should make sure that the woman knows that he or she cares about her safety but trusts her to make the appropriate decisions.

Referral

The minister's job is to link her to the closest specialized services for battered women. Information should be repeated: She should know the name and number of whom she can call in an emergency (e.g., a hotline, the police) and be aware of resources for battered women. If she shows some hesitancy about relying on secular services, then the minister could offer to accompany her to meet with a hotline representative. The minister should reassure her that she or he will be there to assist her with faith questions.

THE MOVEMENT TO SAFETY

The first step in helping a woman move from susceptibility to a life threatening attack to safety is affirming that safety is an appropriate, primary concern. While either the minister or the battered woman may desire to focus on what went wrong with the marriage, why he is battering her, or what she can do to change the relationship so that he stops battering, ministers must actively avoid succumbing to a focus on the relationship. They can say, "We must deal with safety first, relationship issues can come later. But your safety must come first." This affirms that it is okay to spend time focusing on her and her needs, rather than merging her needs with the needs of the relationship. Theological language that affirms safety may be helpful in orienting the discussion to safety (e.g., Jer. 29:11). She should be reminded that she has the right to do what she will do based on what is best for her, not him, not the church, not the minister.

In order to have safety, church support is essential. She needs resources to act. Regardless of her class status, if her abuser controls the money or is the main income source for the household, she will experience a loss of income if she separates from him to achieve safety. Lenore Weitzman (1985) reported a 73 percent drop in divorced women's and their children's standard of living at the same time that there is a 42 percent increase in standard of living for divorced husbands. The church needs to offer concrete help by

providing material support in the short run: through the use of discretionary funds, providing deposits for apartments, identifying items that are
needed and gathering them (furniture, bed linens, dishes, clothes), and financial support for child care as she looks for a job or help with transportation
costs.

Is She Safe?

Battered women are more sensitive to the nuances of the batterer's behavior
than any minister can be. Beware of invalidating their perceptions by minimizing what they sense or assuming that violence is not dangerous because
no one has witnessed it. Battered women are the best experts about their own
situation. If they say they do not feel safe, do not try to talk them out of this
apprehension. It may be easy to trivialize what is said, because life-threatening violence seems incomprehensible to the minister. But this is her reality.
When she says she takes a threat seriously, it should not be shrugged off as
merely a threat. If she thinks that she will be killed if she returns, or if she
leaves, it is not the minister's place to say, Your husband could never do that.
Remember, he has already done many things one might have thought were
unimaginable.

    If there are children, then discussing her care for her children is essential.
What is happening to the children? She is a person in relationship not only
with a partner but also with children who are completely dependent on her to
meet their physical and emotional needs. Are they safe?

    Inevitably the question the battered woman must face is, Should I stay?
Ministers can offer two questions back: Are you safe if you stay? and, Are
there any signs that he has changed? The answer to the question, "Are you
safe if you stay?" is, sadly, no. This is why a referral to a battered women's
program is so essential. *Any* incident of battering can be fatal, leaving either
the wife or the husband dead. Ministers can say:

> I can't make him stop. You can't make him stop. He is responsible for
> his behavior. It is okay to leave the relationship. Safety must be your
> first concern.

Then she can be referred to the closest battered women's program.

Assessing Danger

Assessing danger may involve helping her recognize that the battering has
become more life-threatening and ensuring that neither the minister nor the
victim minimizes the danger she faces. In specific, ministers can ask questions, such as:

Have you or the children been threatened? Does your partner drive recklessly? Can you freely enter and leave rooms? Have you been restrained, grabbed, pushed, choked, hit, punched, kicked, or forced to have sex? Are you able to say no to sexual demands and does he accept the boundaries you establish? What is happening to your children—are they being abused? Have any pets been injured or killed? Has he destroyed any things that you care about?

See Table 4, Assessing Whether Batterers Will Kill, for the life-threatening signals. One counselor of battered women offers this observation about safety:

> The woman is in an imminently life-threatening situation and immediate action is called for where the violence has escalated and any of the following pertain:
> * The partner has begun threatening her life.
> * Having threatened her life in the past, the partner has just brought a knife or gun into the house.
> * The partner has locked her in the house.
> * She sustains multiple injuries with each episode.
> * The partner has killed her pet. (Burstow 1992, 149)

Being alert to the life-threatening situation does not mean that ministers must rescue the victim to help her, but they must honestly assess the situation and help her to do the same. Where the situation is urgent, the minister's responsibility is to speak out of that urgency. If she is unclear, as women in situations of battery often are, then ministers need to provide clarity. We need to review the situation with her and make statements like:

> While it is *your* decision, *no, waiting for a week does not sound safe to me.* I know it is hard, but I want you to look at what has happened. He has already broken your jaw. He has threatened to kill you. He has just brought a gun into the house and could use it at any time. Emma, I really wish things were different, but you can't afford to wait around. The time to act is now. (Burstow 1992, 149–50)

Ministers should err on the side of emphasizing the life-threatening dangers to the woman and ensuring that referral occurs, so that expert assessment by professionals results.

Separation: A Life-Threatening Time

Just because a woman leaves her abuser does not ensure her safety. The time of separation and afterward is extremely dangerous. Violence often intensifies at the point of separation, as the batterer attempts to coerce the woman to return or retaliate against her for rejecting him. Therefore, ensuring her

Table 4: Assessing Whether Batterers Will Kill

1. *Threats of homicide or suicide.* The batterer who has threatened to kill himself, his partner, the children, or her relatives must be considered extremely dangerous.

2. *Fantasies of homicide or suicide.* The more the batterer has developed a fantasy about who, how, when, and/or where to kill, the more dangerous he may be. The batterer who has previously acted out part of a homicide or suicide fantasy may be invested in killing as a viable "solution" to his problems. As a suicide assessment, the more detailed the plan and the more available the method, the greater the risk.

3. *Weapons.* Where a batterer possesses weapons and has used them or has threatened to use them in the past in his assaults on the battered woman, the children, or himself, his access to those weapons increases his potential for lethal assault. The use of guns is a strong predictor of homicide. If a batterer has a history of arson or the threat of arson, fire should be considered a weapon.

4. *"Ownership" of battered partner.* The batterer who says "Death before divorce!" or "You belong to me and will never belong to another!" may be stating his fundamental belief that the woman has no right to life separate from him. A batterer who believes he is absolutely entitled to his female partner, her services, her obedience, and her loyalty, no matter what, is likely to be life endangering.

5. *Centrality of the partner.* A man who idolizes his female partner, or who depends heavily on her to organize and sustain his life, or who has isolated himself from all other community, may retaliate against the partner who decides to end the relationship. He rationalizes that her "betrayal" justifies his lethal retaliation.

6. *Separation violence.* When a batterer believes that he is about to lose his partner, if he can't envision life without her, or if the separation causes him great despair or rage, he may choose to kill.

7. *Depression.* Where a batterer has been acutely depressed and sees little hope for moving beyond the depression, he may be a candidate for homicide and suicide. Research shows that many men who are hospitalized for depression have homicidal fantasies directed at family members.

8. *Access to the battered woman and/or to family members.* If the batterer cannot find her, he cannot kill her. If he does not have access to the children, he cannot use them as a means of access to the battered woman. Careful safety planning and police assistance are required for those times when contact is required, e.g., court appearances and custody exchanges.

9. *Repeated outreach to law enforcement.* Partner or spousal homicide almost always occurs in a context of historical violence. Prior calls to the police indicate elevated risk of life-threatening conduct. The more calls, the greater the potential danger.

10. *Escalation of batterer risk.* A less obvious indicator of increasing danger may be the sharp escalation of personal risk undertaken by a batterer; when a batterer begins to act without regard to the legal or social consequences that previously constrained his violence, chances of lethal assault increase significantly.

11. *Hostage taking.* A hostage taker is at high risk of inflicting homicide. Between 75 percent and 90 percent of all hostage takings in the U.S. are related to domestic violence situations.

If an intervention worker concludes that a batterer is likely to kill or commit life-endangering violence, extraordinary measures should be taken to protect the victim and her children. This may include notifying the victim and law enforcement of risk, as well as seeking a mental health commitment, where appropriate. The victim should be advised that the presence of these indicators may mean that the batterer is contemplating homicide and that she should immediately take action to protect herself and should contact the local battered woman's program to further assess lethality and develop safety plans.

(Barbara J. Hart in Parker, Hart, and Stuehling 1992, section 6: 1–2) safety is not synonymous with her achieving separation from her abuser. Up to 50 percent of men who batter have sought out and continued to beat and otherwise terrorize their wives after they have left. Although they compose only 10 percent of all women, these women report being battered fourteen times as often as women still living with their partners (see Harlow 1991).

Battered women are most often killed when attempting to seek legal redress or when leaving their abusive partner (Parker et al. 1992, I: 7). Women have been killed by their husbands or ex-husbands in front of day care centers when picking up their children; at shopping malls; arriving, departing from, or at work; and at home. Apartments and homes have been broken into, possessions ransacked, children kidnapped.

Ministers can say:

> Maria, I know that you have separated from Pete because of his battering behavior. But this separation is no guarantee that Pete will stop attacking you. In fact, you must recognize that you are still in danger. I want you to be safe. I think you should talk to the battered women's program about exactly how to guarantee your safety.

Ministers can also encourage her, if she has separated from the man who has been battering her, to change the locks on her doors and windows, replace wooden doors with metal doors, install security systems, purchase rope ladders for escape from second-floor windows, make sure that she has smoke detectors and fire extinguishers. Because battered women who leave a relationship usually experience a severe drop in income, financial support from a church's discretionary fund should be offered to help cover the costs of securing a new residence.

She also needs to acclimate herself if she has had to move to a new house or a new apartment: Where are the phones? How does one call the police? Can one dial 911? Where are all the outside doors? How will she ensure that she always has her order of protection on or near her person (in her purse)? Will she make sure that local police departments in the places where she lives, has family, and works all have copies of the protection order? She should talk to her children periodically about the importance of safety. Children need to know how to use the phone. She should teach her older children how to call a relative, a friend, or the police if they hear or see violence.

Because she is in greatest danger if she leaves, she may decide that she is safer staying rather than leaving. The minister must also take this into account. While desiring to support her separation from the abuser, the minister must also be continually aware that the chances are greater that she will be killed if she does leave him. For this reason, the minister must respect her wisdom. She may in fact be safer staying (for the time being) than leaving. She may be attempting to arrange to really run and hide—to escape completely. In the meantime, her self-protective capabilities must be enhanced. And although, in the short run, leaving poses additional hazards, battered women's advocates regard separation as the best way of achieving safety and freedom (see Parket et al. 1992, I: 7). Battered women's programs are best equipped to help her develop plans for safe leave-taking.

Has He Changed?

Has he changed? is a question that may be posed as one attempts to assess a woman's safety. First, a man's promise to change is not a reliable measure of a woman's safety:

> The guarantee of safety in a battering relationship can never be based upon a promise from the perpetrator, no matter how heartfelt. Rather, it must be based upon the self-protective capability of the victim. Until the victim has developed a detailed and realistic contingency plan and has demonstrated her ability to carry it out, she remains in danger of repeated abuse. (Herman 1992, 168–69)

Both the minister and the battered woman may desire to focus on the batter-er's attendance at a counseling program as a sign of change, rather than her own self-protective capability. But participating in a counseling program does not necessarily mean the batterer has or will change his behavior.

Indeed, a man who batters may come in for counseling, not to acquire alternative behaviors, but to get his partner back by conning the counselor and the partner into thinking that changes have occurred. "They use counseling as one more tactic of control—to fool their wives into coming back where they want them" (Jones and Schecter 1992, 109). And women often succumb to the hope that change is occurring. Gondolf and Fisher discovered that women were three times more likely to return home when their partners were receiving counseling (1988, 85). In fact, hands-off battering often increases during this time of counseling. (See Jones and Schecter 1992, 108–10, for a frank discussion of the unlikelihood of men changing by means of their attending counseling programs for violent men.) Battered women's programs can help women gain information about treatment programs for batterers, as well as evaluate whether these programs will bring about the changes in his behavior that will ensure her safety and freedom.

Abusers may promise anything to get her to come back and frequently do not follow through or only go to counseling once. Her return may make the abuser feel even more powerful because of his success in getting her back. A minister's response must proceed from this understanding, remembering that it is important to monitor her danger closely. She may think the abuse has stopped and the man who batters can change solely by promising to change. Several steps can help identify the illusion of safety that the abuser's promises create: reviewing the incidents that she has reported; discussing signs that the abuse has become more life-threatening; identifying controlling behavior from Figure 1, Power and Control Wheel (emotional abuse, using intimidation, using coercion and threats, using isolation) on p. 18; assessing whether the man who batters has actually done anything to implement his promise to change.

Ministers can say:

> I know you hope that he will keep his promise this time. Talking to the battered women's program and making sure you have a safety plan is not a betrayal of your husband. You should view it as insurance for the future.

VALIDATIONS

Abusive behavior is not only upsetting and harmful but also confusing. And her own responses to this behavior may be confusing to her as well. She may be experiencing an intense range of unfamiliar emotions that she never imagined herself feeling. She may fear that she is going crazy. Assuring her that she is experiencing the normal range of reactions to the chronic trauma of battering offers a validation:

> No you are not going crazy, you are reacting as someone would understandably react when experiencing unpredictable, yet ongoing violence. This is something you will learn when you talk with other battered women. You will see that your very intense and unfamiliar feelings are normal.

Learning that there are common responses to trauma can be transformative. She needs to have these overwhelming feelings validated. Ministers can affirm that her reactions are normal:

Let her know that her feelings are normal and understandable, even if they frighten you. Nightmares, phobias, feelings of great fear and terror, paralysis, and helplessness are all typical responses. Battered wives may express great rage and hostility toward their husbands, especially once they have gotten to a safe place where they can afford to vent their anger and hurt. Some even talk of killing the abuser. Respond to the feelings, not the words. Do not ask her not to feel that way or try to convince her that she really loves him. Do not project your own emotional responses to her story or process them with her. (Pellauer 1986, 19)

She may also have a range of somatic complaints:

Chronically traumatized people no longer have any baseline state of physical calm or comfort. Over time, they perceive their bodies as having turned against them. They begin to complain, not only of insomnia and agitation, but also of numerous types of somatic symptoms. Tension headaches, gastrointestinal disturbances, and abdominal, back, or pelvic pain are extremely common. (Herman 1992, 86)

Once removed from the situation of facing ongoing abuse, some of these somatic symptoms disappear. Being able to have a few uninterrupted night's sleep, such as in a battered women's shelter, helps to restore equilibrium. Nevertheless, the chronic pain, depression, nightmares, intense anger, and altered consciousness that occur in the face of an ongoing trauma may take longer to fade. If she was raped by her partner, especially if it was anal rape, then she may have internal injuries besides the ones sustained by the battering.

WILL HE CHANGE?

If a woman asks, Will he change? she is not asking first and foremost a theological question. Will he change? is not a question about conversion, which is always possible, and the answer cannot be solely, Pray for change. Religious issues such as repentance, conversion, the healing of an injured spirit, or an intangible kind of hopefulness should not be addressed without recognizing that these all have practical reverberations. Her question about change is not about spiritual conversion disembodied from his actual behavior.

While these religious considerations are not wrong (Paul, for example, was changed on the Damascus road), they are wrong answers to this question. She is not seeking an answer that affirms change as always possible or that encourages her to pray for change. To feed unrealistic hope in change is to participate in sentencing the woman to a potentially fatal situation. She is asking a practical question: Can he and will he change? (The singularity of the Damascus road conversion ought to be kept in mind.)

A few—too few—abusers may change, may stop using behavior that works for them and instead become sensitized to how others experience this behavior. But encouraging a woman to wait for such conversion is unrealistic and unfair. No one changes unless he wants to change.

Ministers are called to offer both a practical and theological response:

"Maria, the question is not will he and can he change, but until he does, if he does, are you safe?" Moreover, ministers can assert that a woman has the right to demand that her partner change.

A man must be motivated to change in order to stop his battering behavior. The difficulty is that one way that he handles his choice to be violent is through *externalization*, that is, attributing responsibility to events or others outside of oneself. The problem, according to him, is not with him but somewhere out there. While this tendency to externalize may be useful in getting him to begin the process of change (external forces, such as the court mandating him to get counseling or his wife leaving him, now require him to examine his battering behavior), eventually he must develop internal motivation for change in order to end his controlling behavior. "As long as the abuser has not relinquished his wish for dominance, the threat of violence is still present" (Herman 1992, 168). Stopping the physical abuse alone does not make the abuser a changed man. The battered woman can still be miserable because he continues hands-off battering.

> Fernando Mederos of Common Purpose, a Boston counseling program, says that successful change is a process that takes place in three stages. In the first stage, which should occur within a few weeks of starting counseling, the man stops using physical force. "Without this fundamental and immediate change," Mederos says, "nothing else is possible." Then in the second stage the man gives up emotionally abusive behavior, such as intimidation, threats, insults, yelling, and name calling. "Finally," Mederos says, "he must begin to see the woman's point of view and appreciate what she has gone through and what her daily life is like." A man may give up physical abuse and emotional abuse, but until he enters this third stage, Mederos does not consider him successfully "changed." (Jones and Schecter 1992, 111)

Beware of the temptation to gauge change by means of the perpetrator's church-going behavior. Going to church is not enough. When church is brought into the dynamics, it reinforces intense denial because superficially church-going is thought to equal, if not good person, at least good intentions. Going to church, on its own, does not prove that he is no longer going to hurt her. Indeed, if this is new behavior for him, then it may indicate that he is even more threatening, as he is expanding his area of control over her, while also inclining her to suspend her wariness and suspicions.

IMPORTANT: To conclude that she is now safe because he is going to church may interrupt her development of those self-protective capabilities that are urgently needed precisely because she continues to be unsafe. Just as getting sober is not enough, getting faith is not enough either. Ultimately, the question that battered women need to ask is not, Has he changed? but, Do I feel safe to be myself with him? Because of the trauma he has caused his wife or partner, she may not wish to reconcile with him even if he does change and succeeds in relinquishing his wish for dominance. This is her right and her choice.

FORGIVENESS

Another question that often arises in discussions of safety is whether forgiveness of him needs to be granted. Concern about forgiveness is consistent with

Table 5: Distinguishing Forgiveness	
FORGIVENESS IS	**FORGIVENESS IS NOT**
acknowledgment	coerced
attitude	forgetting (amnesia)
able to lead to healing	relieving offender of guilt or responsibility
different between humans and between humans and God	excusing
a process	always necessary
letting go but remembering	a pastoral power
a choice	bargaining
relationship	quick
hope and relief	automatic trust
readiness	a magic prayer
genuine	a wifely duty
empowerment	required so that God will forgive her

her caretaking role of others. She may think or she may have been told that she must forgive him. But healing does not begin with forgiveness.

Forgiveness of the assaultive man is premature if safety has not been ensured. If the trauma is still immediate, forgiveness is inappropriate. NOTE: She cannot forgive unless the trauma is over. In fact, discussing forgiveness may keep the victim from safety.

Forgiveness is a means of restoring the self to wholeness, refocusing negative energy into positive. It requires an articulation of rage, anger, despair, and letting go. She cannot even safely feel this range of feelings if she is still in a relationship with the man who hurts her.

She may substitute a fantasy of forgiveness for the more frightening fantasy of revenge. With the fantasy of revenge, her legitimate outrage and fury over what has happened to her is channeled into a wish for catharsis through retaliation.

> Revolted by the fantasy of revenge, some survivors attempt to bypass their outrage altogether through a fantasy of forgiveness. This fantasy, like its polar opposite, is an attempt at empowerment. The survivor imagines that she can transcend her rage and erase the impact of the trauma through a willed, defiant act of love. But it is not possible to exorcise the trauma, through either hatred or love. Like revenge, the fantasy of forgiveness often becomes a cruel torture, because it remains out of reach for most ordinary human beings. . . . True forgiveness cannot be granted until the perpetrator has sought and earned it through confession, repentance, and restitution. (Herman 1992, 189–90)

Herman's insights into the working of the fantasy of forgiveness help us to identify what forgiveness is and what forgiveness is not. See Table 5, Distinguishing Forgiveness. Forgiveness—when it is appropriate—takes time. Forgiveness may be a part of letting go, achieving distance and perspective on her experience, overcoming self-judgment and self-loathing.

A woman can gain distance and perspective, however, without forgiving her abuser. She should not feel guilty when she cannot forgive. The victimization is not her responsibility, and if she is still in a relationship in which harm is occurring, forgiveness is not appropriate.

> Ministers can help the battered woman see that she can make decisions about safety without considering the issue of forgiveness, by saying, "You must deal with safety issues first; as long as you are not safe there is no place for a discussion of forgiveness."

Postponing the issue of forgiveness does not invalidate her concern, rather it creates the necessary environment for considering such issues—a safe environment when the trauma is over. Only when she is safe and ready can forgiveness even be considered.

Ministers can say to her:

> I know others have told you—or you have a sense—that you must forgive. There will be a time when you may feel ready to forgive. But that is not your task right now. Forgiveness is letting go. Forgiveness is not the medium by which the rest of us can say the issue is closed. None of us has the right to say, "Hurry up and forgive." It often means, "Suffer and don't change." And remember, forgiveness does not mean trusting. (See Fortune 1991, 173–78)

EXITING AND RETURNING

Leaving a man who batters is a complex process. Do not presume the permanency of any exit. "It often takes four or five separations from an abusive spouse before the fantasy of change within the marriage ends and decisive separation occurs" (Hilberman 1980, 1344). Returning to a man who batters should be viewed as a failure neither on the part of the woman nor the minister. In fact, returning after having acted upon her safety concerns changes the woman, especially if she was able to go to a battered women's shelter:

> These women had the courage to leave the first time; they were exposed to alternatives and new ideas; they found out that people outside their homes can and do care for their welfare; they learned that they are not ugly "freaks" with a rare, individual problem. They may return to the men that abused them, but they do not return the same women they were when they left. They know they managed to leave for safety before and they know they can do it again, if nec-

essary. There are people "out there" who want to help them. (Pagelow 1981, 219–20)

Returning can be part of the process of becoming independent. Women should not be made to feel ashamed or isolated if they return. Here the church is an important resource and should continue to offer a variety of ways for women who return to be included so that they do not feel isolated: invitation to church activities, women's groups, Bible studies, involvement on committees, as a deacon are all opportunities for inclusion.

She may have returned for safety reasons; the assaultive man may have threatened a family member or cherished pet. She may sense that she is safer if she returns. Whatever the reason for returning, the minister needs to assure her of the community's and God's support: "You did not reject God by leaving this marriage. God is not rejecting you at this time." The minister should feel secure that she has a safety plan in place without her having to reveal it. The minister might say, "God still wants you to be safe. I hope you talked with the battered women's advocates about how to stay safe. Please remember, you are not alone."

She may have returned for economic reasons. "The most likely predictor of whether a woman can separate permanently from her abuser is whether she has the economic resources to survive without him" (Parker et al. 1992, Appendix G, 32). The reality of women struggling to pay bills, to make ends meet, and to cover any child-care costs, can reignite the fantasy of her partner's change that she abandoned through leaving. Near birthdays and Christmas, her inability to purchase the presents her children desire, while her husband lavishes gifts upon them—and promises to her that he has changed—can precipitate a return. The church needs to offer material support to women after they have left abusive partners so that their decisions about the relationship are not forced upon them by economic realities. When battered women stay with the man who abuses them, the community and especially the church, needs to ask, "What have we done to hinder the leaving process?" And if she returns after leaving, the church needs to ask, "How have we failed her?"

AFFIRMATIONS

As she is encouraged to reach out to the community for assistance, affirmations should be used. Affirmations are an important way of letting her know what her alternatives are. They honor her with self-determination while unequivocally challenging the violence.

> The partner's words and actions daily beat insignificance into the abused woman. . . . We counter by affirming her importance ourselves and by taking the abuse seriously. The message that we need to give and to keep giving is that

the abuse is not trivial, that it matters a great deal, that she matters a great deal. (Burstow 1992, 154)

The minister can affirm what she has done in maintaining the relationship and raising her children, simultaneously identifying her skills and strengths and confirming her own resourcefulness. The minister can honor what has been done to cope with violence without suggesting that it is the only or the best way to respond to the threat of harm that she faces. During this time, she has been incredibly ingenious and determined; she has shown an immense capacity to love; she has been resilient as she scanned the environment. Possible affirmations include:

- The minister should make you-can statements, such as, You can change your life.
- You are not alone.
- Violent behavior toward you is never appropriate or deserved.
- What you experienced was wrong.
- The abuse you experienced was not your fault.
- Abuse is never acceptable.
- You deserve a nonviolent life.
- You are not responsible for the batterer's behavior.
- You have the right to make choices.
- You can make a better life for yourself and your children.
- You have the right to be safe.
- Change takes time.
- No one deserves to be hit.
- You do not deserve to be treated like this.
- You have the right to live free of violence.
- You have a right to have friends.
- You have a right to see your family.
- You have a right and you have the ability to make decisions.
- It is okay to want a normal healthy relationship, but what you have is not okay.
- No one deserves to be battered, abused, or coerced sexually.
- Your first moral responsibility is to yourself and your children.
- It is possible to reestablish control over your life.

For a brief time, as she talks with a minister, she may be experiencing the safety she has lost. The church becomes sanctuary and support. Calling upon this experience of safety, the minister may refer in prayer to a time when this experience of safety occurs in her home, not just in her church home, praying for a time when her community is a sanctuary for her. After giving practical advice, and being thoughtfully responsive, prayer offers an affirmation of the quest for safety as well as an assurance that God is with her and wants her to be safe.

Safety should not be confused with the cessation of violence. Even if she is separated from the man who batters, separation is no guarantee of safety. The most important option for being permanently safe is the one beyond the control of the victim—it is for the man who batters to decide to stop being abusive and controlling. This is the reason for holding the abuser accountable, ending his violent responses, and separating his identity from control and possession of his partner.

5

ACCOUNTABILITY

One day I received a call from a frantic pastor. On the previous weekend, she had assisted a battered woman in escaping to a shelter. But now a distraught husband had repeatedly called her. The husband, also a congregational member, was anxious to locate his wife. Did the clergyperson know where she was? Pastor Ann had responded accurately to the physical violence against the wife by ensuring that she was safe. But now Pastor Ann felt a sense of guilt for having helped, in her eyes, to engineer the escape. She recognized that the man was clearly in crisis, and she saw herself as pastor to each and every member of the congregation.

Rather than understanding how the man's crisis had been precipitated by his need for control, Pastor Ann saw only his crisis and discomfort and wanted to help alleviate it. A crisis of his loss of the one whom he controlled was masked as the loss of love. She wanted to respond in some positive way, and not understanding the man's desperate need for control, she was manipulated into answering his question: Was his wife at a shelter for battered women? Pastor Ann's unfamiliarity with abusers' behavior and her desire to respond to his need, resulted in a serious mistake in judgment: She told the abusive man that yes, his wife was in a shelter. Now, Pastor Ann was frantic from worry that the woman had been placed in danger by this disclosure.

Ministers need to keep the situation correctly framed to avoid being co-opted by the abuser. The appropriate frame is that the abuser has committed a criminal act, and he should not be allowed to evade the consequences of his behavior. Most ministers instead frame the situation as Pastor Ann did—a basically good man is in pain and needs some information. When such information is shared not only is a woman who needs peace handed over to possible violence, but the man's basic assumptions are left unexamined (see Stordeur and Stille 1989, 88). Sadly, Pastor Ann chose a course she thought would be helpful, thereby losing the opportunity to work with the abuser while potentially endangering the woman's life. She also forgot the absolute and essential rule: Do not give out any information about the victim.

WHY BATTERERS SEEK HELP

A man who assaults his partner may approach his minister because he has been feeling distressed, helpless, and hopeless. These feelings may have become so overwhelming that he seeks help. His violent behavior and desire to control, however, are usually not disclosed.

He may be motivated by guilt over his battering behavior or feel contrite about his most recent assault; he may have injured his wife seriously for the first time or harmed his children. "Realizing the impact of his behavior on others may weaken his minimization and denial" (Stordeur and Stille 1989, 74).

He may fear his violence could kill or he has begun to see its effects on his children. His violence may be bringing fewer rewards. In light of the naming by the minister from the pulpit, the man who batters may approach the pastor for help. A social services agency may have referred him. His abusive behavior may be revealed during marriage counseling. Or the minister may have approached the victim, suspecting abuse, and upon it being confirmed, been asked by her to discuss the problem of his violence with the man who hurts her.

He may be seeking forgiveness from the minister for his battering behavior, a forgiveness that ignores his violence and control, thereby allowing him to elude accountability. He is asking the pastor to become a stand-in for the woman he has harmed.

He may seek help because he has begun to experience explicit aversive results of his decision to be abusive—his partner may be threatening to leave, insisting that he go to counseling in order to prevent her from leaving or make possible her return. He may have been arrested for the first time. In order to avoid these aversive consequences, he comes to the minister, hoping for an appeal by the minister to her to return because he has changed. He may want the minister to appear on his behalf as a character witness in court. These are often the times when the batterer brings the clergy into the process of change—precisely to control the clergyperson, resist change, and achieve relief from these consequences. NOTE: Men who batter come to ministers to avoid something worse.

Men batter because it works, producing the desired results without penalty. Intervening on his behalf with his wife to encourage her return continues to allow his battering to work; intervening on his behalf with the criminal justice system shows him that he can still get away with it. In either case, the minister has helped the man avoid the aversive consequences of his own behavior. In so doing, the minister virtually ensures that the abuse will continue.

An abusive man can truly be anguished about what he does and its consequences. He can also be upset about his partner's threat to leave. Nevertheless, this does not mean that he is ready to engage with counselors or clergy in changing his behavior and assumptions. He may appear compliant and placating. His desire is to ensure that the clergyperson is controlled by him, rather than to address his abusive behavior. Or he may be hostile to the minister because he fears the loss of his family or fears having his abusive behavior exposed. Whether through compliance or belligerence, the abuser wants to control the counseling process. Based on his battering behavior, malevolent characteristics need to be ascribed to this interaction, although one would rather ascribe positive characteristics to it.

PASTORAL RESPONSES TO MEN WHO BATTER

The minister's task is "to become an ally of that part of the man that gravitates toward change" (Stordeur and Stille 1989, 80). Being such an ally is fraught with difficulty. On the one hand, the man's desire to control the relationship inclines him to extreme deceptiveness in relationship with authorities, including a minister. On the other hand, the minister's tendency to focus on religious experiences predisposes him or her to believing so-called confessions and accepting words of feigned repentance without requiring any substantive change of behavior.

Conversion from the desire to dominate is neither simple nor fast. What stops the abusive behavior and facilitates change is punitive and logical consequences. IMPORTANT: A minister's response to a man who batters must be guided by these questions: How will this work to make her safe? and, Will this contribute to her being safe or will this help him manipulate her?

Ministry Means Confronting

Working in a constructive way with a man who batters is challenging. Like Jesus' hard sayings, clergy must offer this meaning to his behavior:

I Abusive behavior is a choice, and I hold you accountable for it.

This may feel uncomfortable, but ministering to a man who batters means confronting him. Ministers must also remind themselves that their intervention is not sufficient because hurting women is a crime, and there are consequences for this.

Clergy Self-monitoring

Ministers may hinder a batterer's conversion to nonabusive behavior (both hands-off and hands-on) by allowing themselves to be manipulated by his exquisitely developed controlling behavior. Ministers can be conned because they desire to see both sides. When this happens they will probably hear an anguishing story about how his violence could not be helped and in which the violence is minimized. These stories sound so believable that many forget: It's his behavior, not her characteristics. Ministers need to remind themselves that a criminal act was committed and to say to him, "You committed a criminal act." This response allows one to keep the focus on behavior and not become tormented by either believing that the batterer is really a bad person or that he is such a fine, upstanding, good person. Again, not his characteristics, but his behavior is what matters. Moreover, as in counseling with the woman, the caregiver must identify and be aware of values, attitudes, and feelings that are brought into play in terms of presumed male and female roles and the legitimacy of aggression.

What ministers see is a good man in pain; what they need to see is someone who must face the consequences of his deeds. This is difficult, so self-monitoring of the minister's response is essential. If the minister has been able to establish a relationship with someone at a battered women's service, then a call to get support in standing up to the man who batters can be invaluable.

Beware of Helping Him Manipulate Her

Men who have problems with violence continue battering, abusing, or raping because these activities work for them in many ways. In order for men who harm women to stop, these activities must lose their effectiveness. What would bring this about? Either the rewards of their activities must diminish, or the punishment-deterrent to their actions must become sufficient disincentives to the rewards (or a combination).

In order to create disincentives and accountability, ministers must stop helping him manipulate her. They must also stop relieving him of aversive consequences. Most of the "don'ts" of pastoral care recommended here arise precisely because, unlike traditional pastoral responses, these responses derail manipulation, diminish rewards, and create accountability.

- Do not tell him anything about her.
- Do not collude with the man who batters.
- Do not represent the abuser's needs to the wife.
- Do not attempt to persuade his partner to return to him.
- Do not protect the abuser from accountability.
- Do not become a conduit of communication for either of them.

Do Not Tell Him Anything about Her

Recall the situation of Pastor Ann. The violent man had decided that his need was to regain his wife; only then would this aversive consequence for his behavior be eliminated. The pastor accepted the man's agenda, and the abuser's control of the interaction prevailed. But an alternative response was possible. Pastor Ann could have begun by saying, "I assure you that your wife is safe, but I will not tell you where she is." This speaks to his legitimate anxiety while making it clear that he cannot control his pastor. She could then focus on what should be the primary concern of this parishioner—his use of violence—and what he can do about it. And in focusing on his behavior, they could have worked toward the recognition that his behavior must be the focus. His problem is that he chooses to be violent; the consequence of this choice is that his wife may have sought safety.

Do Not Protect the Abuser from Accountability

External, aversive forces communicate to the abusive man that the rewards of harming a woman are decreasing. At that point, he stands poised on the brink of change. Not wanting to change, he seeks ways of controlling the aversive consequences rather than address his battering behavior. This is the point at which the minister's role can become crucial. A man who has problems with violence may seek an ally who can eliminate the aversive consequences of his behavior. This is precisely what he wants his clergyperson to do. Thus he approaches his minister. (Remember, battering men come to ministers to avoid something worse.)

For instance, an assaultive man may seek his clergyperson's assistance after his wife has fled from him because he assumes that the church's commitment to marriage will favor his—not his wife's—position. He may also expect to have his views of the authoritarian male role biblically endorsed. Although seemingly contrary to pastoral instincts, the minister must refuse to intervene on behalf of a man who hurts women. Such a man learns accountability only when no one intervenes between him and the consequences of his behaviors (Ganley 1991, 217). When ministers plead with the court to reconsider sentencing decisions because the man is an upstanding church member or plead with the woman to return home, their intervention keeps the man who batters from experiencing the consequences of committing illegal acts. They remove one of the external motivations that might begin his journey to discovering internal motivations for change. What appear to be the abuser's needs (to know where his wife is, to avoid criminal prosecution or imprisonment) are not the larger community's needs (to protect victims, to ensure that justice is done, to help someone stop abusive behavior). NOTE: Refusing to intervene should not be confused with refusing to help or to care. The minister can offer much assistance, but not in the form of intervening.

HOW TO RESPOND TO CONTROLLING AND VIOLENT BEHAVIOR

In talking to the man who batters, a minister must speak firmly, judging but not shaming him. A minister can say:

> Your behavior is violent (or abusive). This violence is a problem. It is your responsibility to stop the violence. I believe that you are in control of your own behavior and I care enough about you to hold you accountable for it.

Judging But Not Shaming

In talking with him about his choice to be violent, a minister will want to avoid both euphemisms that communicate an inability to handle the details or a response that shames him and silences him. Nevertheless, ministers need to express a judgment about the behavior as well as support of his struggles:

- "I am here to support you, and I understand your difficulties and struggles. I also want you to know that I think it is wrong to hit or otherwise hurt another person. It is important for you to know that it is wrong, but it is equally important for you to know that I am here to help you." (Stordeur and Stille 1989, 82)
- I am judging your behavior, not your humanity.
- I am not going to desert you, but I am not going to excuse you either. This is not betrayal. Speaking the truth is the best way I can help you.

Nurture Motivations to Change

Many perpetrators may feel self-pity because they feel no one understands, including the clergy whom they see as having sided with the abused. But a minister can say:

- I am on your side as you become a person who does not batter. I am against your battering behavior. I do not believe you should treat your wife as an object that can be battered. But I am in total support of you as you seek to change.
- I am calling you to repent and to change. You will probably suffer in the process of change. You cannot rely on old coping mechanisms that included battering. New life is possible, but it requires work.

Making the Referral

Ministers should avoid counseling the man on their own as the sole response to the crisis his battering behavior has provoked. He may start to feel that he is being persecuted, and thus the minister cannot become the ally with that part of him that wants to change because the part that wants things to stay the same has developed such a distrust. Private counseling does not overcome his social and emotional isolation. Because the counseling remains secret and does not address the shame associated with the secrecy, it reinforces the individual focus rather than encouraging a view that violence is learned and thus can be unlearned. A group works so much better than individual counseling because it undercuts the batterer's denial and minimization. It also makes the behavior public. No matter how special the relationship with the man who batters is, the minister should not fall captive to the fantasy that he or she alone can bring about conversion. Ministers also want to discourage his dependency on the woman by structuring support within the church and the community. This support can affirm new behavior and new relationships.

Ministers must indicate that in order to work on changing his abusive behavior, he requires more help than can be provided individually through the church:

> You have within you the ability and the tools to change, but I am not the person best equipped to help you in this process of change. The violence is your responsibility. Treatment must not focus on your wife (or girlfriend) but on you, so you must go to counseling alone. A group treatment program that specializes in working with men who batter is the best way to receive assistance in changing your behavior. I myself do not work in this field, but I know of a program that can help.

The minister should state clearly to the abuser that he will not offer couple counseling:

> As long as you choose to be violent, you have ruptured the covenantal nature of the relationship. I will not provide marital or joint counseling. There are no relationship issues that we can address until you stop choosing to be violent.

Consult the local resource list. On it should be the name of a program that has already been checked out, one that offers group counseling for batterers with therapists who have experience in treating abusers and that says it works toward ending emotional, physical, and sexual violence. The nearest program may be some distance, but a minister can encourage the batterer that its benefits far outweigh the inconvenience of traveling. Perhaps a friend or a church member could accompany him on the drive if it is an onerous distance.

Addressing His Church-going Behavior

Ministers will need to address with the batterer the issue of whether his partner wants him to continue coming to church. If she does not, then the minister can indicate to the abuser that he could demonstrate his desire to change and his respect for her needs by going to a different church. The minister can guarantee that he or she will continue to see the batterer during this time and even recommend a church for him to attend.

Distinguishing between Remorse and Repentance

It is important to help the man distinguish between remorse and repentance. See Table 6, Distinguishing Repentance. Remorse for batterers is usually a temporary emotion (I'm sorry honey, I didn't mean to hurt you); repentance means commitment to change and actively working to achieve that change.

Table 6: Distinguishing Repentance

REPENTANCE IS	REPENTANCE IS NOT
change of behavior	remorse, easy (casual)
long-suffering	always accepted
regeneration (new start)	always sufficient
accountability	just saying I'm sorry
tied to restitution	freedom from restitution
genuine (there is behavioral evidence that repentance has occurred)	repeating offense
	cheap grace

Remorse is not the final stage for the man who batters, repentance is (Fortune 1991, 183). Ministers will need to remind batterers that promises to change are staples of the batterer's behavior. Concrete actions that signal change count. Indications that there has been a real change in behavior are needed (e.g., Ezek. 18:30-32).

Conversion requires some turning around of behavior, not empty words, but genuine efforts. Conversion needs to include addressing all controlling behavior, such as intimidating or pressuring his partner, "the withholding of financial support, making accusations or threats of infidelity, issuing ultimatums or deadlines for her to 'make up her mind,' using the children as allies against her, and accusing her of not appreciating his efforts to change" (Adams 1988, 193).

Persons who use violence against a partner must take action to repent. Ministers might brainstorm exactly how to do repentance. The list, when completed, should include these components:

• I am responsible for repairing what I broke.
• I need to tell the truth about what I have done.
• I must acknowledge that harm has been done and say, I'm sorry, and mean it.
• I must change. And after changing, I must make restitution.

Another brainstorming tool is identifying what repentance is and is not. This list might resemble that in Table 6 found above.

Provide Affirmations

Affirmations for the battering man include:

• You have a potential for change. This requires a commitment.
• There comes a point when blame, recrimination, and past anger and resentment are no longer reasons to cling to old ways of living. There is new life!

- You can help yourself. You can begin to change. You can stop what you have been doing.
- You must ask for help. You need to understand that getting help requires hard work.
- By not stopping this abuse, you may go to jail or lose your family. By stopping the abuse, you begin to work toward a relationship that has meaning rather than control, but you must love your partner's freedom and integrity more than your need to control her.
- There is a part of you that desires a better life, a healthier relationship. I am an ally of that part of you that gravitates toward change, but I will continue to judge that part of you that resists change and hurts another.
- That you need others is a positive sign of connectedness, a sign of relationship, but relationships are not built on control and authoritarian behavior.
- Repentance—active change of wrongful behavior—brings about the healing of the human spirit.
- "Get yourself a new heart and a new spirit! . . . Turn, then, and live!" (Ezek. 18:30-32)

ARREST AND ACCOUNTABILITY

The most effective way to stop battering and also protect the victim is through arrest and prosecution. Any sort of counseling that is provided should be done in conjunction with vigorous prosecution for violation of the law. Suspended sentences fail to affix blame. Diversion to a counseling program should occur after an adjudication or admission of guilt. Community sanctions are important to keep domestic violence from being seen only as a private matter; it is a crime.

Criminal prosecution should occur in every case of woman-battering for several reasons: It alone establishes that battering is criminal activity not interpersonal problems gone awry. It alone imposes accountability, which is usually lacking when legal sanctions are not invoked.

Because prosecution has been the most successful deterrent to the rewards of violence, ministers should encourage the use of the criminal justice system. It can send the message that the man who batters is breaking the law and that it must stop. Ministers can help the man who hurts a woman see that an arrest offers an opportunity for repentance because it creates a form of accountability:

1. Recognizing that the sinfulness lies not in the arrest but in the acts of harm committed by the abuser and the concomitant secrecy forced upon the victim.

2. The arrest provides the opportunity for true repentance, a turning around, if the accused will confess and seek counseling to change his behavior.
3. Ministers can indicate to the accused that they will accompany him through the legal system—not to protest his innocence, nor to claim that as a loyal church member the acts alleged to have been committed by him were inconceivable, but to ensure that he gets help.

For the batterer, the process of going through the criminal justice system may be full of stigma. Perhaps no one until now has told him that what he has done is wrong. He may be shocked by his arrest. If he is white he may feel indignant; if he is a person of color, he may be concerned about how he will be treated.

When the abusive behavior of a man becomes public knowledge because of prosecution—this is the moment for supporting him through the process of change that such public knowledge and accountability should help precipitate. Unfortunately, this is often the moment when the minister does not want to be seen publicly supporting the batterer. Ministers may not want to be identified publicly with someone going through the criminal justice system's process of arrest and adjudication. A failure of nerve may occur if the minister actually gets the man who batters to go to court and then realizes that he or she should appear with him. As with the batterer, secrecy and privacy may feel more comfortable than public scrutiny and association with battering behavior.

The man who batters should not be rejected or stigmatized by the congregation and neither, for that matter, should the minister who encourages the batterer to cooperate with the criminal justice system. Otherwise, the batterer's desire to avoid the aversive consequences of his behavior is accommodated.

The minister can say:

> What you did was wrong. You need to get counseling to learn more appropriate ways of responding. I know that court-mandated counseling is often the only way that men who harm their partners actually participate fully in the counseling program. Through the prosecution for your offense, you will be offered the chance to change, to learn more effective ways of interacting, and to respect your partner. I will support you in this.

Ministers can also remind the man who does feel stigmatized by the prosecution for his assaultive behavior:

You have an option for avoiding future legal consequences of your battering behavior: Change your behavior.

KEEP SAFETY ISSUES PARAMOUNT

The point of separation is a dangerous time. A man who achieves control through battering his female partner desperately wants her back. Several important guidelines need to be followed: Watch for a life-endangering batterer; do not minimize the wife's concern for safety; guard personal safety; put it all together.

Watch for a Life-endangering Batterer

Some men who batter are suicidal; others will murder. See Table 4, on p. 76, Assessing Whether Batterers Will Kill.

> While it is true that all batterers are dangerous, some are more likely to kill than others and some are more likely to kill at specific times. . . . Considering these factors [in Table 4] may or may not reveal actual potential for homicidal assault. But *the likelihood of a homicide is greater when these factors are present.* The greater the numbers of indicators, the greater the likelihood of a life-threatening attack. (Hart in Parker et al. 1992, VI, 1)

Recognize that "I can't live without her," and "I refuse to live without her" may be threats to her life (Stordeur and Stille 1989, 106).

Confidentiality and His Violent Behavior

If the minister suspects, in meeting with the batterer, that he is going to be violent again, then she or he needs to tell the man that the police and his partner will be alerted, and the minister should follow through. If the minister knows that the man has hurt his children, then this man should be encouraged to self-report his abusive behavior to Child Protective Services in the minister's presence. Let him know that it is a clergyperson's ethical duty to report child abuse and that the batterer's choice is not whether it will be reported, but who will do the reporting.

Do Not Minimize the Wife's Concern for Safety

His word alone is no guarantee that the violence indeed has stopped. Remember, her safety depends on her self-protective capabilities, not on his promise to change. Do not dismiss as harmless any act of violence; do not discourage the victim from being concerned about the suicidal potential of her partner.

Guard Personal Safety

Anne Ganley discusses the safety concerns of counselors who work with men who batter (1981, 97). In brief, a batterer is more likely to attack someone helping his partner than someone helping him. Ministers will probably be working not only with the abusive man but also with his victim and, hopefully, will have referred her to a battered women's program. Thus such ministers' safety risks may be greater than if they were working with the battering man alone. Ministers should meet with batterers when they know that there are other people on the church property. Wherever they sit, they should have easy access to their telephone and the door.

Putting It All Together

Pastor Mike performed a marriage for Howard and Jasmine. A few months later, suspecting abuse, he arranges to meet with Jasmine. He asks her several general questions, then moves toward more specific questions about Howard's behavior. Yes, Jasmine confirms, Howard has been hurting her. But, she said, he was getting counseling for both his alcoholism and his battering behavior. They were dealing with it, she explained. Pastor Mike makes it clear to Jasmine that she should feel free to call him if she felt scared or concerned about Howard's behavior. He asks her if he has her permission to discuss this with Howard, and she agrees.

Pastor Mike then meets with Howard, and asks him about his battering behavior. Howard indicates that he is working on it at counseling. Knowing that they had drawn upon community resources, Pastor Mike feels reassured. Pastor Mike's plan has several strong parts to it:

- It recognizes that couple's counseling was not an appropriate forum for raising the issue of battering or for addressing it once it was identified.
- Conversation with the man who batters only occurs with the victim's permission.
- It offers no guarantee of confidentiality to the perpetrator.
- The minister does not attempt to mediate the batterer's concerns to the victim.

Nevertheless, Pastor Mike's plan also had several weaknesses:

- Pastor Mike should have ensured that Jasmine was in contact with a battered women's program and that she was participating in group counseling session. Her safety is not guaranteed by Howard's getting counseling. He should have also informed Jasmine that through counseling Howard might acquire more "hands-off" battering skills that would replace "hands-on battering" but would continue to be controlling and threatening.

- Pastor Mike should have asked Howard for more information on the counseling program he was taking part in. He needed to assess whether this was in actuality a batterer's program. Was he in a group for batterers with therapists who have experience in treating abusers? Were words such as "conflict-resolution" or "communication problems" used to describe their approach in their brochures? If so, this would not be a reliable program. Or did the counselors name violence, and say they work toward ending emotional, physical, and sexual violence? To ascertain that this program did so, Pastor Mike could have asked for a contact person at the counseling agency, and inquired into the nature of the program while also confirming Howard's participation and commitment.
- He should have established that the next incident would be reported to the police, and that Howard would not try to pressure Jasmine into withdrawing any charges that would be filed against him.
- Pastor Mike should have discussed with Howard the ideas of male authority or dominion that undergirded his controlling and abusive behavior and that Jasmine had the right to have other associations besides the relationship with her partner.

SCRIPTURE AND MEN WHO BATTER

An abuser can twist just about anything to justify his use of violence, claiming as reasons for his actions the adding of mushrooms to a pizza, the vacuuming of a room at the wrong time of day, the taking of a job, or the refusal to have sex. How much more salient are selected texts from the Bible about women being obedient or sinful! He believes that he has the right to control her and looks to the Bible to find those places that appear to confirm this right. To be sure, he must selectively proof text, clinging to the Bible as imprimatur for his privilege and control, but the Bible seems to have passages that severely circumscribe women's role. Biblical authority adds to the woman's confusion and the man's authority.

In holding the abuser accountable, the minister can also hold out the Bible as a source of affirmation that change is possible, that God wants him to change, and that Jesus offers a model for noncontrolling behavior. Using clerical authority, the minister can state clearly that clinging to the Bible as yet another explanation for his choice to be violent is simply unacceptable. The minister can also help him interpret his duties toward his partner as religious duties: to get out, to stay away from her, and not to look to her for caring. Opening up his understanding of Scripture could include exploring the texts discussed on the following pages, but such an exploration should not substitute for ensuring community responses to the batterer's behavior; rather it should complement these responses.

Peter's Denials and Witnessing

In focusing on the one who denied Jesus (John 18:15-27), yet who was a "witness to the resurrection" (Acts 1:22; see 1:16-25; 2:14-40), the minister establishes the dialectic between denial and change. The minister can establish many thematic parallels. For example, Peter denied his relationship with Jesus; the men who batter deny that they have a controlling relationship determined by their behavior. The cock crowing for the abusers may have been the criminal justice system. And so forth.

Peter is a model of someone who did wrong yet also did much good, moving from denial to leadership through his behavior. As with Peter's three denials and his subsequent remorse, the abusive man has the pain of knowing his behavior is wrong. Like Peter he can move through it. Claiming that he loses control denies his actual choice of violence. Is not this denial of identity similar to Peter's denial of his identity as one of Jesus' disciples? Yet, Peter changed from a man who denied to a man who witnessed to the resurrection; by changing from a man who denies that he is in control, to acknowledging his desire to control, the man who batters can become a witness to another kind of resurrection—the resurrection of a man who adopts nonviolent, noncontrolling ways of interacting with the person he loves.

IMPORTANT: Do not offer the promise that a resurrected relationship will result, because the decision about that must rest with the woman he has harmed.

The Woman Taken in Adultery

Because extreme jealously and accusations of infidelity characterize most men who batter, the woman taken in adultery (John 7:53—8:11) is an ideal text for exploring issues around accusations, infidelity, sin, and their own relationship to Jesus. What is Jesus writing on the ground? Jesus may have been asking them to examine themselves: Why do you think this woman is adulterous? What is your need to believe this? Are you experiencing feelings that she usually protects you from? Why do you want to harm this woman? Like the scribes and Pharisees who accuse the woman in the biblical text, batterers avoid focusing on their own behavior. Instead they are outraged by hers. Jesus, however, does not succumb to this misfocusing. A minister could ask, What is it that Jesus might be writing on the ground for you, the abuser, to read?

> You are in control.
> You are responsible for your behavior.
> I call you to accountability.

The minister can encourage him to visualize this story for himself, so that he sees that Jesus is always standing between him and his victim.

Submission and Love

Ephesians 5:20-33 figures in many abusive men's justifications for their violence. Pairing it with a passage now used in many marriage ceremonies (1 Corinthians 13) can help open up a discussion of what marriage relationships should be. The minister might begin by having the batterer discuss his sense of what Ephesians 5 means. Has he himself ever used it when harming his wife? Has he ever justified his battering behavior toward his wife by referring to this text? What exactly is the husband's role in Ephesians 5? Is there male privilege and control in this passage or not? Who is to be the model for his behavior? How would he characterize Jesus' relationship to the church — as controlling and abusive, or inviting and loving? Can the batterer point to any text in the Bible that condones physical abuse of one's spouse?

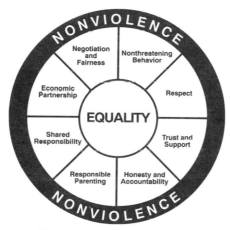

Figure 3: The Equality Wheel

NONTHREATENING BEHAVIOR
Talking and acting so that she feels safe and comfortable expressing herself and doing things.

RESPECT
Listening to her nonjudgmentally • being emotionally affirming and understanding • valuing opinions.

TRUST AND SUPPORT
Supporting her goals in life • respecting her right to her own feelings, friends, activities, and opinions.

HONESTY AND ACCOUNTABILITY
Accepting responsibility for self • acknowledging past use of violence • admitting being wrong • communicating openly and truthfully.

RESPONSIBLE PARENTING
Sharing parental responsibilities • being a positive nonviolent role model for the children.

SHARED RESPONSIBILITY
Mutually agreeing on a fair distribution of work • making family decisions together.

ECONOMIC PARTNERSHIP
Making money decisions together • making sure both partners benefit from financial arrangements.

NEGOTIATION AND FAIRNESS
Seeking mutually satisfying solutions to conflict • accepting change • being willing to compromise.

The Equality Wheel has been adapted from a wheel developed for the Domestic Abuse Intervention Project, Duluth, Minn. Used by permission. On the original wheel, the text appears within the spaces between the spokes.

Once Ephesians 5 has been discussed, and his justification of abuse by citing that passage is found to be at odds with the model of Jesus' relationship with the church, discuss Figure 3, The Equality Wheel. In order to have a healthy relationship with a woman, the batterer must be able to treat women as equal and independent human beings. Is he willing to do this? The minister might suggest that misreading Ephesians 5 is one way of seeing in a mirror dimly, but embracing the meaning of 1 Corinthians 13 and understanding the equality wheel is one way to see his partner face to face, equal to equal. Suggest that he write various passages from 1 Corinthians 13 onto appropriate sections of the equality wheel. Tell him he must respect her more than his need to control her. He must always ask himself, Is what I want fair?

The batterer can pray to God for help in accepting the way others act and feel and thank God for his ability to change. In their proactive responses to men who hurt women, ministers announce, "I'm not going to abandon you; I'm going to hold you accountable." Only with accountability can there be new life.

6

SUFFERING AND THEOLOGY

The Christian trauma survivor is left with the question of how she is to respond to Christian ethical and theological issues, such as repentance, forgiveness, suffering, and redemption. When violence against her or her children has become the norm, these Christian issues enormously complicate her thoughts about leaving the man who hurts her. When she turns to Christianity for solace and insight—bread for her soul—it may feel instead that she is receiving heavy stones (Matt. 7:9). Before she can feel comfortable turning to a specialized service for battered women for help, she must come to terms with seeking solace and safety—this bread—outside of her family and her church.

THEOLOGICAL CONSTRICTION

One of the effects of ongoing trauma and coercive control is psychological constriction. Not only is the abused woman experiencing a narrowing of relationships, activities, thoughts, and memories, but she also is living in a climate of danger. "When the victim has been reduced to a goal of simple survival, psychological constriction becomes an essential form of adaptation" (Herman 1992, 87). In the face of this constriction, she may cling tenaciously to her religious faith, but it, too, is being forged in the crucible of confusing and demeaning abuse. "All the psychological structures of the self—the image of the body, the internalized images of others, and the values and ideals that lend a person a sense of coherence and purpose—have been invaded and systematically broken down" (93). Her religious faith may survive, but not unscathed by this invasion and destruction.

Unlike the moral struggles often portrayed in traditional ethical discourse, in which the individual is presumed to be "free and self-directing" in considering "a wide range of choices" (Cannon 1988, 2), the moral sphere in which battered women must make their ethical decisions is constricted and dangerous. A battered woman's interpretative process occurs in the midst of chronic trauma, not safety and security.

Listening to her explain how she has tried to fit her traumatic experience into her religious understanding, one will learn how her religious crisis has been so lonely, unattended, and unsupported. Within this constricted life she

103

has worked hard as a theologian, attempting to understand her experience, her God, and her savior. In the face of physical violation, she may still understand that her soul remains her own. But just how does this soul relate to this injured body, to the man who is causing her suffering, to the outer world, and to the faith community? As she must subordinate her interests to the control of the man who hurts her, she may attempt to subordinate her reality to certain religious precepts that encourage endurance of the violence rather than challenging it, that focus on her spiritual characteristics rather than his behavior. What she faces is theological constriction.

Despite the limited goals she has adopted in order to survive within the coercive control of her abusive partner, despite the fact that "the future is reduced to a matter of hours or days" (Herman 1992, 89), she makes faith statements all along. She finds hope in the smallest things, hoping against hope that any sign of benevolence on his part indicates that he is changing.

> We often talk about battered women's slide toward hopelessness as a factor in their staying with an abusive man. But hope can be as great a hook: hope for change, hope for improvement, often in the face of overwhelming odds. As one woman expressed it, "I go to bed pretty beaten down at night, but my soul gets back up in the morning." The fact that battered women maintain a home and often care for children as well as caring for the abuser, while they are being physically attacked and threatened, testifies to the depth of their resiliency and strength. (Browne 1987, 86)

The resiliency of finding hope in even the smallest signs—hoping that a change will occur, that she can make a change occur, that the abuser is changeable by something outside of himself—enlarges small signs of possible change out of proportion. Judith Herman comments, "Through the practice of dissociation, voluntary thought suppression, minimization, and sometimes outright denial, [battered women] learn to alter an unbearable reality" (1992, 87).

The Christian victim is equipped with formidable tools for altering an unbearable reality. Because a part of a woman's preparedness to live on her own may involve a series of departures and returns, religious precepts carry different meanings at different times. When she resolves to stay she looks for affirmation of this decision; she may find this affirmation in religious notions such as suffering, forgiveness, and a just God who exacts punishment. When she resolves to place her safety first and recognizes that this probably involves leaving, she searches, too, for affirmation of this. Although images of the exodus from slavery, of Mary's magnificat proclaiming that the proud have been scattered, the mighty put down, and those of low degree exalted, might speak to her situation, they are often not seen as applying to her own liberation from violence. The constriction and isolation that she has experienced are reflected in this theological constriction as well; she attempts to find ways for her understanding of suffering, forgiveness, and her image of God to be transported from one situation, staying, to another, separating. In leaving, or in contemplating leaving, she cannot easily dispense with those concepts that have given her staying theological meaning. How does she then accommodate them?

THEOLOGICAL PROVOCATION

The victim of a violent man believes one of two things: The world, God, and the church do not protect the weak (offering only stones); or the world, God, and the church do protect the weak, but only if they are deserving (yes there is bread, but it is not for her). Either she has been abandoned by God or she is being punished by God.

That she looks for the cause of her suffering in herself is a logical step. The effort to understand the cause of one's victimization is a healthy sign. It is an effort to regain some semblance of control over one's life and environment, to regain that which was lost in the chronic trauma. Focusing on her self may provide some sense of optimism because she thinks that she may have some control over the situation, but she is participating in story telling rather than truth telling.

Story telling can occur on the theological level, as well, in which she continues to focus on her characteristics (her sinfulness) rather than his behavior (his violence). The theological level also offers a variation on this story telling that maintains the focus on characteristics, this time focusing on God's characteristics (punishing or abandoning) rather than the behavior of the man who hurts his partner.

She may feel that God is punishing her and look for causes in herself (I haven't been a good wife, I did something wrong when I was a teenager), including religious causes (I haven't been a good enough Christian, so God is punishing me). The focus is on God or herself instead of the actual cause of suffering: her husband's decision to exercise control and use violence. Because she cannot change God, she struggles to change herself. The seemingly appropriate religious answers fit not only with the story-telling focus, which our culture and the batterer encourage the woman to adopt (it is somehow her fault, she can change him), but also with images of God as ultimate punisher, who keeps a tally card of infractions. God assumes the characteristics of the batterer: The One who causes suffering, the One who is harsh and arbitrary, and who offers stones instead of bread.

Actually, the man who batters causes suffering, is harsh and arbitrary, stoning her rather than nourishing her. Her husband is responsible for her suffering. The movement from story telling to truth telling will include a religious dimension that addresses this idea of theological provocation. Her minister can help her see that the cause of the violence lies with the abuser. It is his decision to hurt her, not God's. The care provider can say:

> I believe that people use their freedom to hurt others. I believe that people can exercise their freedom to stop hurting others. Is this battering God's will? No, this is the will of the abuser. It is not God's will for you to suffer. I don't believe that God is punishing you. You should pray to God about what you feel you are being punished for, to relieve you of this terrible burden. But don't believe that God is punishing you. Remember what is written in Jeremiah 29:11: "For surely I know the plans I have for you, says the LORD, plans for your welfare and not for harm, to give you a future with hope."
>
> You have begun to realize God's will in seeking help, and asking a battered women's program for help is another step in the unfolding of God's will for you to be safe. God weeps for what you are experiencing. God is brokenhearted by the abusive behavior. I believe God does not want you to be hurt.

MAINTAINING THE FOCUS ON BEHAVIOR

Although it is impossible here to summarize every religious crisis experienced by women who suffer violence from their partners, focusing on behavior rather than characteristics is a central aspect of appropriate response. When, for example, she worries that she is committing the sin of pride by worrying about herself, she is focusing on her characteristics. She needs to focus on the freedom of choice of the man who is harming her. This consideration moves us from her characteristics to his behavior. She may think that she is meant to endure the beatings (again, her characteristic); she might fruitfully explore whether God is the God of change and whether this change includes anti-battering behavior by her partner.

Thus, focusing on his behavior rather than her characteristics is a theological task as well as a pastoral task. Although not a simplistic formula for responding to the religious crisis of battered women, this insight offers an anchor in the midst of a crisis with competing interests (his and hers), the threat of serious injury or death, and immense emotional conflicts. Maintaining a focus in the swirling tempest of these urgent demands may seem impossible. Yet, the behavior-not-characteristics guideline can be a constant help in responding. It has appeared in earlier discussion of religious issues. For instance, the answer to the question, When is the covenant broken? needs to be based on behavior—the covenant was broken by his abusiveness. Repentance means in part that all battering behavior is stopped. If the batterer does not stop his abusive behavior, there may be remorse, sometimes strong and anguished (and maybe never), but it is not repentance. Consider as well the confusion about the perpetrator's demands for forgiveness of his behavior by the victim; the woman thinks she must have the characteristic of being forgiving. But this is not so, and any discussion of forgiveness before she is safe, that is, before the battering behavior is stopped, disregards the needed focus on behavior.

In encouraging a woman hurt by a man to call battered women's service providers and maintaining the focus on the batterer's behavior, the minister can help to reverse the effects of theological constriction:

> You do not have to mediate your abuser's relationship with God; it is his behavior and his alone, and he must be accountable for it. If God would not give you more than you can handle, why do you think God would give your abuser more than he can handle? You may be confusing your testing with his. At the moment, God is calling you across the Red Sea to safety. You have told me how your partner has pursued you, like Pharaoh's army, seeking you out. It is for him to decide whether he will stop pursuing you and begin to examine his relationship with God. God is there for him, just as God is there for you. His relationship to God is his responsibility, not yours.

SUFFERING AND THE SURVIVOR'S MISSION

The focus on her characteristics rather than his behavior occurs when she attempts to understand his behavior by focusing on the meaning of her suffering. Because truth telling about his decision to be violent is so difficult, holding onto the redemptive meaning of suffering combines all of the story-telling survival mechanisms with the incredibly powerful gospel story of Jesus' crucifixion.

Perhaps no Christian concept is so thoroughly misapplied toward and by victims of abuse than that of christological suffering. This concept becomes interpreted as, Christ suffered, and I must suffer, too, to be like him. Christ's physical suffering, interpreted as redemptive for all, is thus claimed as a model for those whose partners hurt them. The victim's struggle for meaning seemingly has had to be squeezed into a sacrificial model in order for her experience to be meaningful. How else can she account for her undeserved suffering?

The suffering servant model may likely keep victims from establishing safety as their first priority and keeps them distracted from a focus on behavior. How understandable that battered women might gravitate to the suffering servant sacrificial model to cope with the abuse. As the primary caretakers and nurturers of the family, women's self-development is often sacrificed to the family and considered redemptive for all involved, including the woman (Pearson 1989, 99). For women, the perceived Christian emphasis on sacrifice matches the way in which girls are taught to consider others rather than themselves, to be self-sacrificing in a social situation. The religious meaning of sacrifice is thus layered on top of the social view of women as sacrificial.

The idea that bodily suffering is spiritually redemptive for others also intersects with the traditional Christian notion of denial of the body. Thus, women's bodies are separated from the idea of being redeemed in and of themselves, of having bodily worth or bodily integrity. Pastoral care providers must spend time exploring the concepts of suffering that may keep women in abusive situations.

Moreover, for a woman whose assaultive partner is HIV-positive, the likelihood of contracting AIDS from her partner may indeed make her sacrifice literal by likely contracting the fatal disease from him. If she is pregnant or breast feeding, then she can pass the virus on to their offspring.

Numerous battered women report that their clergy encouraged them to return to their abuser and offered the model of Christ's suffering. In addition, some battered women themselves interpret their suffering as redemptive because they think they are helping their husband whom they see as suffering. Both Christ's suffering and the way that abuse works for the abuser are misunderstood in these instances.

Several approaches for releasing her from her focus on suffering are possible. Each offers movement from suffering to redemption. While each involves refocusing the meaning of the women's suffering, these responses honor the women's theological stance. Beginning with theological positions that have helped them survive, ministers can explore just how these same positions can be applied to enable women to seek safety as a part of their theological purpose. Central to refocusing is never losing sight of the assaultive man's behavior and maintaining an understanding that "many men who batter are genuinely sorry afterward and promise it won't happen again. Unfortunately, however, his being sorry has nothing to do with his not battering again" (Men Stopping Violence, 4).

Is Suffering Succeeding?

Is the goal of redemption being achieved, or is it closer to being achieved by the continual abuse to which she is subjected? The woman's suffering will neither heal the abuser nor protect him. Her concern about the meaning of suffering continues the focus on her characteristics rather than his behavior. Thus the abuser is not held accountable. In the absence of such accountability, her suffering cannot be redemptive because he is not saved from that which is destroying him, her, and their relationship—his decision to be violent. Whereas Christ's suffering may be seen as redemptive, suffering from abusive men does not redeem, indeed it guarantees that the violence will continue. The abuser, in not being called to account, misses the opportunity of redemption. The minister can say, "Loving him may make you want to stay with him, but in the long run the most loving thing you can do for each other is to separate, at least temporarily" (NiCarthy 1982, 53).

Jesus' Suffering Was Unique

For women who have survived battering by clinging to their suffering as theologically meaningful, an exploration must begin with their sense of Jesus' suffering. Was not Jesus a unique individual? Thus, his suffering is unique.

Did not Jesus suffer once and for all so that no one else would ever have to suffer as he did? Jesus' suffering liberates us from having to follow this path. But some women may take Paul's statement, "We suffer with him so that we may also be glorified with him" (Rom. 8:17), as a further legitimation. We may infer from this passage that suffering in life is necessary and thus unavoidable. Several responses building on this belief are possible. If suffering in life is necessary and unavoidable, then she is freed from seeking for some explanation in her past that explains her current suffering. None is needed because suffering is the Christian's lot.

Nevertheless, one cannot conclude from this that all suffering is necessary and unavoidable. The amount of suffering does not matter, and this being so, some suffering can well be meaningless. Her suffering, for instance, is unnecessary and avoidable. Her suffering results from injustice. The best response to suffering that is unjust is to struggle against it.

Paul does not imply that solely enduring suffering is the goal. Earlier he speaks of "a spirit of slavery" that "falls back into fear" versus "a spirit of adoption" (Rom. 8:15). Your relationship to God does not free you from suffering in life; we all suffer. But your relationship means that you can be released from slavery, from enslavement to the control of a batterer. The question is not, Can you endure this suffering? Obviously you have. The question is, Should you have to endure such suffering? And nowhere in the Bible does it say that your partner has the right to hurt you, and that you have the duty to stay and be harmed.

Refocus the woman's emphasis on the importance of her suffering as following in the path of Jesus by exploring the differences in their suffering. Jesus' experience of suffering was finite; if nothing changes her suffering is potentially infinite. The minister might point out that Jesus was only crucified once. And while that was a painful, tragic, and awful day, Jesus never had to face that day again. What about her situation? Sometimes beatings and the accompanying abusive treatment may last for hours. (A majority of the women interviewed by Dobash and Dobash experienced at least two attacks per week. Of these, 25 percent reported that the violence lasted from 45 minutes to over 5 hours [Dobash and Dobash 1979, 120].) How many Good

Fridays must she endure before she, like Jesus, never has to face those days again?

Refocus the woman's emphasis on the importance of her suffering in the model provided by Jesus by contextualizing Jesus' suffering. Jesus' suffering is a result of his living in and challenging an evil, violent world. Jesus suffered as a result of others' actions. Some would argue that the phrase "Jesus suffered" misconstrues that experience, so building on it by saying, "Jesus suffered so that we would not have to," does the same. They argue that suffering is not something that Jesus did, but something that was done to him (Marlena Cardena-Griffin reflecting on Oseick 1986, 73 [discussion, April 1991]). Suffering was not the goal but the world's response to living out the truth. Jesus' suffering then was a consequence of his decision to live the truth and someone else's decision to stop him from living the truth. What truths is someone else preventing her from speaking? The truth about her experience in this relationship?

Jesus Halted the Suffering of Others

When Jesus had the opportunity to stop or prevent suffering he did. Often, the suffering individuals were women, the woman whose bleeding would not stop, the woman taken in adultery, the Samaritan woman. If Jesus were in the room, would he say to her, "Yes, continue suffering as I did," or would he say, "Stop suffering! Whenever I could, I stopped suffering, and your suffering can be stopped"?

The minister might encourage her to think about the idea that Jesus is with women in battered women's shelters. The meaning of suffering is refocused by exploring what happened in the Garden of Gethsemane. There we find not the acceptance of suffering, but resistance to it. Whenever a person has a please-let-this-cup-pass-away-from-me feeling, she or he is likewise resisting suffering.

But the departure from the garden raises the specter of betrayal and a betrayer. If the battered woman is the suffering servant, then what role does the man who hurts her hold? His behavior has a role in her experience, just as Judas's behavior had a role in Jesus' crucifixion. Someone does not suffer independent of someone else causing the suffering. This dynamic allows us to focus on the ones who are causing the suffering, the Roman government that wanted to control Jesus and the Jews, and the betrayer, the Judas, the covenant breaker.

Instead of allowing the concept of suffering to remain static by focusing only on her, establish the causes of the suffering and discuss the behavior of the betrayer. Someone made Jesus suffer. Someone is making you suffer. Three groups of people made Jesus suffer: strangers who were violent, friends and strangers who did not stop the suffering, and a betrayer who was Jesus' friend. In the wake of Christ's physical suffering, this betrayer is said to have repented.

In the case of wife abuse, the betrayers are husbands. Their abuse is not called a betrayal—although it should be—and they have not repented sufficiently to stop the violence. Strangers and friends are not stopping the violence either.

The minister can say:

> We need to think about your husband as a betrayer when he batters you. In doing this, the possibility is created for talking about his possible remorse and helping him do something about his remorse that isn't either suicidal or likely to cause more violence toward you. We are wrong to focus on your suffering as though that were all that is going on. Your suffering is the result of someone else. We must engage in truth telling, we must acknowledge the role of your partner's behavior in causing this suffering. Otherwise we have the story wrong.

The meaning of suffering can be refocused by examining the meaning of Jesus' ministry—the prophetic call for concrete acts on behalf of the suffering. The Bible is written from the perspective of the powerless. The arrogant are put down, the idolatry of the powerful is challenged.

> Your suffering is not God's will, battering is not God's will. Your husband is being idolatrous in his controlling behavior. The Bible tells of the struggle for freedom from the cruel and powerful. This is an important message for you.

Jesus' Resurrection Offers Change

Battered women literally die at the hands of their abusers—one every six hours in this country. Refocus the meaning of suffering by emphasizing the resurrection and the paradigm of movement from suffering to death to resurrection rather than static suffering. The minister can say:

> Let Jesus off the cross. We are a resurrection people. Let yourself off the cross. Your suffering should be over too. Because of Jesus you do not need to die to experience the meaning and power of resurrection. If you don't get off the cross, however, you very well may die.

In the case of battering, the death of Jesus is the metaphor for the death of the marriage as it now exists (see Eilts 1988). The resurrection is the new possibility of a relationship without violence, either with or without the man who batters.

Refocus the suffering by raising the issue of witness. The past twenty years of work with battered women has demonstrated two valuable lessons. First, when victim-survivors speak out about their experience of being abused, their courage helps others break the silence. As we know, breaking the silence is the initial step to ending the abuse. Second, when victim-survivors speak together, like the disciples gathered together after Easter, mutual assistance and revelation can occur.

Judith Herman calls this "the survivor's mission" which occurs in alliance with others: "Where there is no way to compensate for an atrocity, there is a way to transcend it, by making it a gift to others" (1992, 207). A survivor's mission involves recognizing that she has been a victim, understanding the effects of her victimization, and then transforming the meaning of this victimization "by making it the basis for social action" (207). Herman observes that "although giving to others is the essence of the survivor mission, those who practice it recognize that they do so for their own healing" (209). If the battered woman has been a part of a battered women's support group, then she will probably have discovered that indeed she does have knowledge that can help others. If she has not, then she needs to make this discovery in the presence of other survivors.

Ministers can say:

Go out into the world and witness about the resurrection, about a new life free from violence. You begin to be saved and to save others, when you are released from the cross and proclaim that no one should be forced to tolerate abuse.

No More Suffering Is Necessary

Finally, the meaninglessness of suffering needs to be discussed. If there is no meaning to the suffering, or if her traditional interpretation of suffering is now meaningless, are we perhaps suggesting to her that her past beatings were in vain? Are we denying her an interpretative framework that made sense out of her experience? No, not at all. If the repositioning of the meaning of suffering and the christological model produces the anguish that her suffering has been meaningless, one way to respond is to say that her past suffering has brought her to the point of being able to say, This is enough.

Being long-suffering should not be confused with being actively engaged in change. Whatever you have suffered, you know somewhere, by talking to me, and exploring this issue, that you have suffered enough. Yes, you can mourn for the self that had to endure this suffering. Mourning the losses such suffering caused is appropriate. But no more suffering is necessary. The question now is not, What is the meaning of those beatings? but How do we create the reality by which those beatings can be stopped? To continue to suffer is, in part, to deny the validity of your past suffering. You must have compassion for the self that has suffered. You can say, "It is enough. It—the suffering—is finished. I deserve a life free of violence. My moral responsibility must be, at this moment, to myself. It is time to move onto new life."

A COMMUNITY THAT OFFERS BREAD NOT STONES

A relationship exists between a community's response to violence and one's experience of God. If a community responds to a woman's harm by immediately saying, This shall not happen again, and then puts into place the mechanism for ensuring that this is so—such as court-mandated counseling and reinstitution of the charges if battering occurs—in other words, if a community responds by saying, You matter, a caring and responsive God has been made present. But when a community appears uncaring, failing to intercede after beating upon beating, the absence of response echoes on many levels, including the divine level.

When a woman wonders where God was in her suffering, we need to remind her that she has been forced to ask this question because her community deserted her. Her theological constriction arises because we have allowed isolation to go unchallenged, her trauma to be ever-present, rather than being able to safely secure it in the past. The minister can say to her:

You feel abandoned by God partly because you have been abandoned by your community. So far it may seem your community has been either unable or unwilling to protect you, and it is understandable that you should feel abandoned and left to fend for yourself in a situation where you need the help and care of others. It is our responsibility to help you believe in a meaningful, rather than meaningless, world. That you are unable to believe this denotes our failure, not yours. Lack of community response to batterer's harm has rendered the world meaninglessness; you cannot be expected to reconstruct this conditional world—and conditional God—on your own. But your community can help protect you, and in doing so it can help to make God present to you. As one representative of that community, and as someone who has talked with others about the problem of woman-battering, I can tell you that we want you to feel that you are a part of this community, and that we wish to make God present to you. A battered women's shelter is the space that exists to confirm what we say: We want you to be safe.

I am sorry that the community has failed to help you feel God's grace: We have given you a millstone around your neck rather than the tools for making bread. It is the responsibility of the community to ensure that women are safe from men who batter. I believe that God wishes for your safety, not your death.

Prayer is an appropriate response to violence. But it is not the only response. Offering a prayer, and only a prayer, when first approached by a battered woman would announce an inability to help and a desire to dematerialize the problem. But after making appropriate referrals, praying for strength, for safety, for healing, for God's presence, can join together the material and the spiritual, providing a model for her of a spirituality that does not attempt to escape this tragic world.

By articulating and acting upon a theological and spiritual framework that accommodates her reality while seeking to expand the theological constriction that occurred in the face of trauma, a minister communicates: "Your reality is meaningful. Your safety is essential." The minister acknowledges her struggle to squeeze sustenance from the stones that she has been given, but offers her instead the bread of life.

CONCLUSION: CREATING A RESPONSIVE CHURCH COMMUNITY

Naming the violence, ensuring safety, and creating accountability do not take place in a vacuum, but occur within the midst of community. For many women who suffer violence, and for the men who hurt them, the church is a vital, if not major, source of community experiences. It may respond negatively, shunning and stigmatizing the battered woman and the battering man. The church community may think it is taking a neutral stance in response to the problem of woman-battering, but neutrality results in ignoring or dismissing the problem. As Judith Herman observes, "All the perpetrator asks is that the bystander do nothing" (1992, 7). Bystanders, by their nature, side with the perpetrators by allowing violence to go unchallenged. The alternative is for the church community to determine that it will enhance the positive environment for naming and accountability that you are creating in your ministry.

CREATING CHURCH RESOURCES AND EDUCATIONAL PROGRAMS

The church community's responsiveness can be enhanced in a number of creative ways. Below are suggestions that have proved helpful in more than a few congregations:

- Ensure that your church library has books on woman-battering, child sexual abuse, and rape. Publicize the acquisition of books such as Marie Fortune's *Keeping the Faith,* Ann Jones and Susan Schecter's *When Love Goes Wrong,* and Ginny NiCarthy's *Getting Free* in your church newsletter.
- Subscribe to newsletters of local and national programs, especially *Working Together to Prevent Sexual and Domestic Violence* (from the Center for the Prevention of Sexual and Domestic Violence, 1914 N. 34th St., Suite 105, Seattle, Washington 98103).
- Start a study group of religious issues and woman-battering, publicize the group's conclusions so that those being victimized have access to theological interpretations that challenge the abuser's reality.
- Develop curricula on woman-battering and child sexual abuse for Sunday school classes, or inquire as to whether your denomination has done so. Encourage them to do so, if they have not.

- Provide educational resources for teens, including the exploration of the issue of dating violence (see Levy 1990). Arrange a joint youth group program with other churches of several week's duration on issues associated with dating violence. (College chaplains should make sure that they address the issue of dating violence in sermons and other communications to students.)
- Have speakers from secular service agencies, such as battered women's shelters, child protective services, and rape crisis centers, speak to church groups. Devote more than one session to the topic, to convey the seriousness and extensive nature of the problem.
- Ensure that the staff at the church are trained and that any pastoral care providers have gone to workshops and acquired relevant information.
- With the church council or session, develop a church policy about battering, child sexual abuse, and marital rape. "List all the behaviors that are abusive. Note those that are clearly illegal in your state, those that are physically dangerous, those that are psychologically dangerous, those that are demeaning, those that are sexually abusive, and those that are destructive to relationships or self-esteem. Declare the intent of your congregational leaders to end such behavior patterns and encourage healthy lifestyles" (Kowalski 1988, 202).
- Refer to ending violence in the home through litanies and prayers as well as in sermons.
- Include hotlines and battered women's shelter phone numbers in bulletins and newsletters, and on church bulletin boards. Also publish other resources available to congregational members.
- Conduct a Bible study that includes 2 Samuel 13, Judges 19, and other passages that feature violence against a woman (see Trible 1984).
- Show films about battering, especially *Broken Vows: Religious Perspectives on Domestic Violence,* available from the Center for the Prevention of Sexual and Domestic Violence (address on p. 115).
- Provide healing services for victims and survivors.
- Create liturgies for lament and anger.

RESPONDING TO THE VICTIM AND THE ABUSER

The congregation should not ostracize victims or abusers. Instead, bring them into the community and provide a model of mutuality. Support the woman in moving beyond the trauma, and support the man as he accepts the consequences of his behavior. This can include becoming a part of the woman's support group as she extends her network of contacts, or accompanying the man to any possible judicial hearings about his behavior, not to advocate for him, but to support him as he goes through the process by which his accountability is established.

- Ensure that the church's social activities are not solely couple-oriented.
- Create a fund to pay the emergency shelter expenses of victims of woman-battering, and develop resources for other things a family might need in an emergency: child care, clothes, food, and so forth.
- Assist women who have to leave their violent mate in finding a place to live and helping to furnish it.
- Encourage survivors who wish to speak about their experience to do so, and provide opportunities within congregational activities for such speaking to occur. This affirms what Judith Herman calls the "survivors mission." But beware of strip-mining survivors, exploiting their words rather than respecting them.
- Ensure that the women are accompanied through the family or criminal court.

PREVENTIVE EDUCATION

Offer preventive education for children and teenagers on subjects, such as sexuality, mutuality, communication, and assertiveness skills as well as curricula developed especially for church communities around sexual violence (see Fortune 1984, Reid and Fortune 1989, and Reid 1994).

- Arrange for self-defense classes for church members and assertiveness training for women.
- Actively help to define healthy relationships and identify what abusive ones look like.
- Ensure that one aspect of premarital counseling is a discussion of violence. This counseling can help identify conflicting assumptions about the acceptability of violence, issues around the control of money, and other aspects of controlling behavior and authoritarian positions. Look for signs of a controlling personality. Questions to pursue could include: How are you critical of each other? Do you insult each other? What was your parents' marriage like? What do you think Ephesians 5 instructs about marriage? Premarital counseling should include meeting with each individual separately and pursuing questions such as, Does you fiancé constantly criticize you? Insult you or call you names? Limit your ability to see your own friends or family? Threaten to beat you or commit suicide? Ask you to account for every minute of your time? If this is a second marriage you might address the issue of controlling behavior in the first, and assess whether the woman is still recovering from post-traumatic stress disorder.
- Create baptismal and marriage vows that affirm nonviolence. "Include antiabuse vows in the marriage ceremony. Rather than wait to see whether one spouse will abuse the other, it would be a better preventive

measure to alert people at the beginning that certain behavior is wrong. Ask them to vow not to do violence to one another or to their children. That way, an abused spouse will not feel guilty for seeking help, nor will she blame herself for the violence. She has already been assured by her spouse's vow that violence will not be used. If it is, he has betrayed his own word" (Kowalski 1988, 205).

- Expand the church's metaphors for God so that God language does not appear to communicate any imprimatur for fathers and husbands to be authoritarian.

SUPPORTING COMMUNITY RESOURCES AROUND BATTERING

When filling out the resource sheet, some needs of the community will likely be identified that are not being met. Assess how the church can be a catalyst in helping to create the needed resources, especially if there is no shelter or battered women's program in the community.

- Collect items for the nearest shelter for women escaping violent partners (diapers, shampoo, food, furniture). Ask the shelter to identify its needs. By collecting items, the church is not only providing valued contributions but also alerting members that a special resource exists, even if it is miles away.
- Encourage mission support to groups helping battered women.
- If your community has a shelter, see if they are pursuing the creation of second-stage shelter (housing of six months to two years to which the formerly battered woman graduates after her shelter experience) and help them in developing this valuable resource.
- Lobby with local, state, and national legislators, encouraging support of local programs.

All that the perpetrator asks of the church community is to be a bystander, that is, to do nothing. As Judith Herman observes, "He appeals to the universal desire to see, hear, and speak no evil. The victim, on the contrary, asks the bystander to share the burden of pain. The victim demands action, engagement, and remembering" (1992, 7–8). In becoming a responsive church community to woman-battering, the church informs both the perpetrator and the victim: We will not be bystanders to violence. At that point, in response to woman-battering, its work becomes life-affirming and life-saving.

APPENDIX
HANDLING AN EMERGENCY CALL

While many ministers may never receive a call from a woman who states that her husband hit her (or threw her against the wall or raped her), some ministers *will* receive a call like this. In a crisis call, the minister's responsibility is to respond to immediate needs.

Figure 4, Flow Chart for Crisis Calls, provides a model for handling a crisis call of this nature. Its purpose is to provide a structure for a conversation and not necessarily script a dialogue, in part because the caller's situation can vary greatly. Depending on the answers to these questions, the minister will recognize an extremely life-threatening situation or a crisis that has momentarily passed. Responses, therefore, need to reflect these differing circumstances.

> Whether or not the woman is in physical distress, your most important task is to remain calm and in control of the conversation. Panic can easily be contagious. One of the easiest ways to prevent, control, or mask your anxiety is to talk slowly and breathe slowly and evenly. If you remain calm and talk in a concerned manner, you can then do the other essential task of crisis intervention—*helping the woman define and label her immediate needs and concerns.* (Cooper 1976, 22)

If a minister is called by a battered woman immediately after a beating, she or he should be prepared to ask the following questions:

- Are you or your children in danger now? How long do you have to talk? Is the violence over?
- Where is the batterer now? Where are the children now?
- Have you called the police? (Remind her to get the police officers' names.) Do you want me to call the police?
- Do you want to leave and can you do so safely? Do you have a place to go?

Since response time may be critical, the flow chart—adapted from one used by staff members of a hotline—identifies most of the essential questions to be asked. The purpose of the flow chart is to provide guidance for clergy during emergency calls, which are more likely to happen once the issue of abuse has been raised in the congregation; to leave the victim the right to make her own decisions, to decide what options she wants to follow, but to encourage her to contact the local hotline; to provide ways of assessing medical needs. Battered women often minimize the damage inflicted on their bodies, and have actually developed a high threshold for pain.

> To help her ascertain the extent of her injuries, questions such as the following should be asked: Are you dizzy? Is there swelling? Where were you hit? Are you bleeding? What did he use to hit you?

She may be in physical and emotional shock, or suffering from a chronic state of exhaustion. Her decisions are compromised by her own physical state and the nearness or distance of the batterer.

If the phone call is interrupted by the abuser's violent entry, *call the police.* In addition, "if a woman is in imminent danger, *but cannot leave her home safely*, tell her that you will call the police. Explain to her that . . . it may take some time for them to arrive. BE PRACTICAL! Suggest locking the door, barricading it with furniture, escaping through the door, a window . . ." (Cooper 1976, 26).

IMPORTANT: The minister should not go to the home unless accompanied by the police. In fact, when a minister is called because of a crisis situation, no matter whether it is apparent that the battering has stopped, do not go to the home unless accompanying the police.

Encouraging her to contact the closest battered women's program is an important step. The minister will be alerting her to several things simultaneously: 1) She is not the only one who has experienced this, others have as well, and resources exist to address their specific needs; 2) There are alternatives to staying in the house; 3) Her safety is paramount.

At this time of emergency, what is needed is an immediate response, rather than any attempt to require her to think in terms of long-term decisions. The inclusion of the emergency flow chart in a book on pastoral care is not an attempt to make the minister into the Lone Ranger. Yet, being equipped for intervention is a necessity in the wake of naming violence.

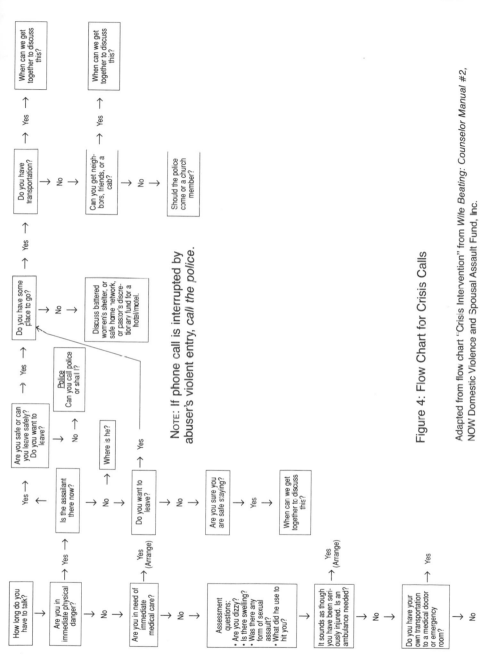

Figure 4: Flow Chart for Crisis Calls

Adapted from flow chart "Crisis Intervention" from *Wife Beating: Counselor Manual #2,* NOW Domestic Violence and Spousal Assault Fund, Inc.

BIBLIOGRAPHY

Books useful for further study are annotated.

Adams, Carol J., and Marsha Engle-Rowbottom.
1991   "A Commentary on Violence Against Women and Children in Rural Areas." In Marie M. Fortune, *Violence in the Family: A Workshop Curriculum for Clergy and Other Helpers.* Cleveland, Ohio: The Pilgrim Press.

Adams, David.
1988   "Treatment Models of Men Who Batter: A Profeminist Analysis." In *Feminist Perspectives on Wife Abuse,* ed. Kersti Yllo and Michelle Bogard. Newbury Park, Calif.: Sage.

Bowker, Lee H.
1983   *Beating Wife Beating.* Lexington, Mass.: Lexington Books.

Bowker, Lee H., Michelle Arbitell, and J. Richard McFerron.
1988   "On the Relationship between Wife Beating and Child Abuse." In *Feminist Perspectives on Wife Abuse,* ed. Kersti Yllo and Michelle Bogard. Newbury Park, Calif.: Sage.

Browne, Angela.
1987   *When Battered Women Kill.* New York: Free Press.

Browne, Angela, and Kirk R. Williams.
1989   "Exploring the Effect of Resource Availability and the Likelihood of Female-Perpetrated Homicides." *Law and Society Review* 23, no. 1: 75–94.

Burstow, Bonnie.
1992   *Radical Feminist Therapy: Working in the Context of Violence.* Newbury Park, Calif.: Sage.

Campbell, Jacquelyn C.
1986   "Nursing Assessment for Risk of Homicide with Battered Women." *Advances in Nursing Science* (July): 36–51.

Cannon, Katie.
1988   *Black Womanist Ethics.* Atlanta, Ga.: Scholars Press.

Carlin, Kathleen.
n.d.   "Defusing Violence: Helping Men Who Batter." Available from Men Stopping Violence, 1020 DeKalb Avenue #25, Atlanta, GA 30307.

Cooper, Barbara.
1976   *Wife-Beating. Counselor Training Manual #2 "Crisis Intervention."* Ann Arbor, Mich.: NOW Domestic Violence and Spousal Assault Fund, Inc.

Crenshaw, Kimberlé.
 1992 "Whose Story Is It, Anyway? Feminist and Antiracist Appropria-
 tions of Anita Hill." In *Race-ing Justice, En-gendering Power: Essays on
 Anita Hill, Clarence Thomas, and the Construction of Social Reality*, ed.
 Toni Morrison. New York: Pantheon Books.
"Developments in the Law—Legal Responses to Domestic Violence."
 1993 *Harvard Law Review*. 106, no. 7: 1498–1620.
Dobash, R. E., and R. P. Dobash.
 1979 *Violence against Wives: A Case against the Patriarchy*. New York: Free Press.
Eilts, Mitzi N.
 1988 "Saving the Family: When Is the Covenant Broken?" *Abuse and Re-
 ligion: When Praying Isn't Enough*, ed. Anne L. Horton and Judith
 A. Williamson. Lexington, Mass.: Lexington Books.
Family Violence Prevention Fund.
 1992 "Domestic Violence in the Immigrant Community: The Problem."
 The Network News (July/August): 1, 3–4.
Finkelhor, David, and Kersti Yllo.
 1983 "Rape in Marriage: A Sociological View." In *The Darker Side of
 Families: Current Family Violence Research*, eds. David Finkelhor,
 Richard J. Gelles, Gerald T. Hotaling, Murray A. Straus. Beverly
 Hills, Calif.: Sage Publications.
 1985 *License to Rape: Sexual Abuse of Wives*. New York: Holt, Rinehart,
 and Winston.
Fortune, Marie.
 1984 *Sexual Abuse Prevention: A Study for Teenagers*. New York: United
 Church Press.
 1987 *Keeping the Faith: Questions and Answers for the Abused Woman*. Essential for every church library and every Christian battered woman.
 Contact the Center for the Prevention of Sexual and Domestic Violence (address on p. 115) for copies.
 1991 *Violence in the Family: A Workshop Curriculum for Clergy and Other
 Helpers*. Cleveland, Ohio: Pilgrim Press. The "how" and "what" of
 providing educational resources to the faith community.
 1992 "Wings of Eagles and Holes in the Earth." In *Preaching Through the
 Apocalypse: Sermons from Revelation*, ed. Cronish R. Rogers and
 Joseph R. Jeter, Jr. St. Louis, Mo.: Chalice Press.
Fortune, Marie, and James Poling.
 1993 "Calling to Accountability: The Church's Response to Abusers." In
 Clinical Handbook of Pastoral Counseling, Vol. 2, eds. Robert J.
 Wicks and Richard D. Parsons. New York: Integration Books.
Freire, Paulo.
 1972 *Pedagogy of the Oppressed*. New York: Penguin.

Ganley, Anne L.
 1981 *Court-Mandated Counseling for Men Who Batter: A Three-Day Workshop for Mental Health Professionals*. Washington, D.C.: Center for
 Women Policy Studies.

1989   "Integrating Feminist and Social Learning Analyses of Aggression: Creating Multiple Models for Intervention with Men Who Batter." In *Treating Men Who Batter: Theory, Practice, and Programs*, ed. P. Lynn Caesar and L. Kevin Hamberger. New York: Springer Publishing.

1991   "Perpetrators of Domestic Violence: An Overview of Counseling the Court-Mandated Client." In *Violence in the Family*. See Fortune 1991.

Gondolf, Edward W., with Ellen R. Fisher.

1988   *Battered Women as Survivors: An Alternative to Treating Learned Helplessness*. Lexington, Mass.: Lexington Books.

Harlow, Caroline Wolf.

1991   "Female Victims of Crime." *Bureau of Justice Statistics*. U.S. Department of Justice.

Herman, Judith Lewis.

1992   *Trauma and Recovery: The Aftermath of Violence — From Domestic Abuse to Political Terror*. New York: Basic Books. A path-breaking and definitive book on the trauma of abuse and healing from it.

Hilberman, Elaine.

1980   "Overview: The 'Wife-beater's Wife' Reconsidered." *American Journal of Psychiatry* 137, no. 11 (Nov.): 1336–47.

Horton, Anne L., and Judith A. Williamson.

1988   *Abuse and Religion: When Praying Isn't Enough*. Lexington, Mass: Lexington Books.

Jones, Ann, and Susan Schecter.

1992   *When Loves Goes Wrong: What to Do When You Can't Do Anything Right. Strategies for Women with Controlling Partners*. New York: HarperCollins Publishers. An indispensable book for women whose partners are abusive and for anyone helping abused women.

Kaschak, Ellyn.

1992   *Engendered Lives: A New Psychology of Women's Experiences*. New York: Basic Books.

Kowalski, Judith A.

1988   "Developing a Religious and Secular Partnership." In *Abuse and Religion*. See Horton and Williamson 1988.

Lerner, Harriet Goldhor.

1988   *Women in Therapy*. New York: Harper & Row.

Levy, Barrie.

1990   *Dating Violence*. Seattle: Seal Press.

Lobel, Kerry, ed.

1986   *Naming the Violence: Speaking Out About Lesbian Battering*. Seattle: Seal Press.

Luepnitz, Deborah Anna.

1988   *The Family Interpreted: Feminist Theory in Clinical Practice*. New York: Basic Books.

Men Stopping Violence.

n.d.   "Questions You May Have About Men Stopping Violence — For Partners/Former Partners of Batterers." Atlanta, Ga.: Men Stopping Violence.

Miller, Jean Baker.
1976   *Towards a New Psychology of Women*. Boston: Beacon Press.
Newsom, Carol A., and Sharon H. Ringe.
1992   *The Women's Bible Commentary*. Louisville: Westminster/John Knox Press.
NiCarthy, Ginny.
1982,   *Getting Free: A Handbook for Women in Abusive Relationships*. Seattle:
1986   Seal Press. A step-by-step guide for a battered woman on how to make decisions and what to consider.
1987   *The Ones Who Got Away*. Seattle: Seal Press.
Oseick, Carolyn.
1986   *Beyond Anger: On Being a Feminist in the Church*. New York: Paulist Press.
Pagelow, Mildred D.
1981   *Woman-battering: Victims and Their Experiences*. Beverly Hills, Calif.: Sage.
Parker, C. Joan, Barbara Hart, and Jane Stuehling.
1992   *Seeking Justice: Legal Advocacy Principles and Practice*. Harrisburg: Pennsylvania Coalition against Domestic Violence.
Pearson, Carol S.
1989   *The Hero Within: Six Archetypes We Live By*. San Francisco: Harper.
Pellauer, Mary.
1986   "Counseling Victims of Family Violence." *Lutheran Partners* (July/ August): 17–20.
Randall, Teri.
1990   "Domestic Violence Intervention Calls for More than Treating Injuries." *Journal of the American Medical Association* 264, no. 8 (August 22/29): 939–40.
Reid, Kathryn Goering.
1994   *Preventing Child Sexual Abuse: A Christian Education Curriculum for Children Ages 5–8*. Cleveland, Ohio: United Church Press.
Reid, Kathryn Goering, with Marie M. Fortune.
1989   *Preventing Child Sexual Abuse: Ages 9–12*. New York: United Church Press.
Russell, Diana.
1982,   *Rape in Marriage: Expanded and Revised Edition*. Bloomington and
1990   London: Indiana University Press.
Schecter, Susan.
1982   *Women and Male Violence: The Visions and Struggles of the Battered Women's Movement*. Boston: South End Press.
Stacey, William A., and Anson Shupe.
1983   *The Family Secret: Domestic Violence in America*. Boston: Beacon Press.
Statman, Jan Berliner.
1990   *The Battered Woman's Survival Guide: Breaking the Cycle*. Dallas: Taylor Publishing Co.

Stordeur, Richard A., and Richard Stille.
    1989   *Ending Men's Violence against Their Partners: One Road to Peace.*
            Newbury Park, Calif.: Sage.
Switzer, David K.
    1986   *The Minister as Crisis Counselor.* Nashville: Abingdon.
Trible, Phyllis.
    1984   *Texts of Terror: Literary-Feminist Readings of Biblical Narratives.* Phil-
            adelphia: Fortress Press.
U.S. Congress.
    1990   Senate. *Women and Violence: Hearings Before the Senate Committee on
            the Judiciary.* 101st Cong., 2d sess. 117 (testimony of Angela
            Browne, Ph.D.).
Walker, Lenore.
    1984   *The Battered Woman Syndrome.* New York: Springer.
Weitzman, Lenore.
    1985   *The Divorce Revolution.* New York: Free Press.
White, Evelyn C.
    1985   *Chain Chain Change: For Black Women Dealing with Physical and
            Emotional Abuse.* Seattle: Seal Press.
Yllo, Kersti, and Michelle Bogard, eds.
    1988   "Treatment Models of Men Who Batter: A Profeminist Analysis." In
            Feminist Perspectives on Wife Abuse. Newbury Park, Calif: Sage.
Zambrano, Myrna M.
    1985   *Mejor Sola Que Mal Acompanada: For the Latina in an Abusive Rela-
            tionship.* Seattle: Seal Press.
Zorza, Joan.
    1991   "Woman Battering: A Major Cause of Homelessness." *Clearinghouse
            Review.* Special Issue: 421–29.

LOCAL RESOURCES

Battered women's program hotline number _____

Nearest women's shelter name _____

  Contact person _____

Police _____

Sheriff _____

Ambulance _____

Hospital emergency room _____

Child Protective Services _____

Rape hotline _____

Information and referral _____

An order that protects a woman from her abusive male partner is called:
    peace bond   order of protection   injunction   restraining order

Where the woman can obtain it _____

Counseling for violent men is available at _____

District attorney's office telephone _____

  Contact person _____

Legal assistance _____

Medical help _____

Hospital social worker _____

Alcohol abuse counselor _____

Drug abuse counselor _____

Department of Social Services _____

Social Security office _____

Child support enforcement _____

Services for the elderly _____

Emergency care for mentally and physically disabled _____

Respite care for care givers _____

Emergency and financial assistance _____

Local Planned Parenthood or other reproductive health

   counseling center _____

Vocational rehabilitation (jobs training) resource _____

Lawyer _____

Doctor _____

Child care _____

Food pantry _____

Clothing _____

Public housing office _____

   Contact person _____

Public transportation _____

Emergency transportation _____